KB272324

다시 길 위에서

On the Road Again

작은 글 모음

다시 길 위에서
On the Road Again

조철형 지음

두 인
DOOIN BOOK

다시 길 위에서
On the Road Again

조철형 지음

- Signetics, LG반도체, 하이닉스, 충북 테크노파크 반도체센터, HASCO 근무
- 2004 대통령표창 수상(대통령 노무현)
- 2006 한국반도체협회 산업발전공로상 수상(협회장 황창규)
- 저서 : 회복으로의 여정, 내 마음의 수채화

Note) · 이 책에 사용된 성경구절은 『성경전서 개역개정판』을 사용 하였습니다.
　　　· 책 제목 『다시 길 위에서』는 창세기 13:14~18에서 영감을 받아 붙였습니다.

다시 길 위에 섰다

『회복으로의 여정』 출간 이후 세 번째로 엮은 것이다. 벌써 그렇게 되었나 나도 놀랍고 의아하다. 그래도 일상의 삶을 감사함으로 바라보는 것은 은혜 아닐까?

길 위를 걸으며 느낀 감정을 담담한 마음으로 적어보았다. 일상을 꾸준히 솔직하게 기록하고 싶다는 생각으로 써 본 글이다. 무엇보다 나와 주위를 다시 한번 돌아볼 수 있는 시간이었음에 감사하다.
그저 주위로 물이 넘쳐 흘러 잔잔한 감동이나마 전해지길 바랄 따름이다.

"내게 능력 주시는 자 안에서 내가 모는 것을 할 수 있느니라" 라고 말씀하신 것처럼 남은 여정도 담대히 길 위를 걸어가련다.

아내와 가족에게 감사하고 나를 사랑하는 모든 이에게 감사하다.

조 철 형
Steve Cho

Chapter 2 야고보서 묵상

Chapter 1

작은 글 모음

I 가 - 바

갈팡질팡

할아버지 마음은
이런 때 어땠을까

살아생전 작기장
제목이던 갈팡질팡

그 마음 전이되어
나도 갈팡질팡

잡다한 번뇌에 흔들리다가 내가 중2 시절 돌아가신 할아버지(조종술)의 기억
이 새로워지다 _ 2510

Undecided

I wonder—

in moments like this,

how did my grandfather's heart feel?

In the small notebook he kept while alive,

the title he once wrote was this word:

Undecided.

That feeling crossed over,

passed into me.

And now,

I stand here as well—

Undecided.

Shaken by many small, tangled worries, the memory of my grandfather—
who passed away when I was middle school—
returns, not as something gone, but newly alive.

감사

선배님 후배님
감사합니다

지나온 세월도 감사하고
즐거운 지금도 감사합니다

만나면 배움이 있고
만나면 각성이 있고

무지의 깨우침에 감사하고
위로의 한마디에 감사하고

정이 오감에 감사하고
다른 시각에 감사하고

이 땅에서의 한 해가
또 저물어 가고 있습니다

Thanks

To my seniors,
to my juniors—
thank you.

I'm thankful for the years we've passed,
and thankful, too, for the joy of this moment.

When we meet, there is learning.
When we meet, there is awakening.

Grateful for the moments
when ignorance is gently shaken awake.
Grateful for a single sentence of comfort.

Grateful for the warmth of coming and going
Grateful for seeing the world
through another set of eyes.

Another year on this land
is quietly drawing to a close.

선배님 후배님 건강하시고
하고자 하는 일 다 이루시고

내일은 보다 나은 미래로
붉은 태양을 마주 하소서

May you be healthy, both seniors and juniors.
May all that you set your hearts on
find its way to fulfillment.

And tomorrow, toward a better future,
may you stand and face the rising red sun.

Written in Yangjae, after a year—end gathering with seniors and juniors.

갑자기

나는 또 울었다

홀로 온 출장 길 어느 단골식당에서
젊은 알바 학생 울 딸 얼굴과 겹치며

갑자기 흐르는 눈물 멈추질 않는다
울 딸 생각에 지나온 삶의 회한悔恨에

하나님 회복시켜 주세요
나에게 눈물주신 하나님의 뜻대로

불쌍히 여겨 주세요
제발

나의 의지 하나님

SF 출장 길; 한식당(Sutter 707)에서 혼밥 한 그릇 먹다가 울 딸 생각나 적다
_ 2307

Suddenly

I cried again.

On a business trip, alone, in a familiar restaurant,
a young part-time worker's face
overlapping with my daughter's.

And suddenly, the tears begin to fall—
and they will not stop.
Thinking of my daughter,
thinking of the life already lived,
the weight of regret pressing in.

God, please restore me.
According to Your will—
the God who placed these tears in my eyes.

Have mercy on me.
Please.

My will, my God.

Written in San Francisco, on a business trip— while; eating alone in a
Korean restaurant as Sutter 707, thinking of my daughter.

까치

젊은 시절 불리운 별명
지금까지 쭈욱

성정이 까칠한 탓일까
부르면 즐거운 탓일까

나의 성姓을 붙여 부르면
배倍가 되는 즐거움

너도 나도 파안대소破顔大笑

그 이름
까치

Magpie

A nickname given in my younger days—
and somehow, it stayed.

Was it because my nature was a little sharp?
Or because calling it out
always brought a laugh?

Add my family name to it,
and the joy doubles.

You laugh.
I laugh.
Faces opening wide with shared delight.

That name—
Magpie.

Yes.
I hereby announce my nickname to the whole wide world.

개의 생각

이 세상에 많고 많은
젠체하는 인간님들

속마음 따로 겉 모습 따로
탐욕과 위선 미소로 포장한 채

반가우면 꼬리 흔들고
느낌오면 싸질러 버리는

솔직한 우리가 낫지 않은가
적어도 가식은 없지 않은가

개의 시선으로 바라본 오늘의 세계— 동네 벤치에 다리 하나 들고서 거리낌없
이 볼 일 보는 개를 바라보다가 뜬금없이 개소리 한마디 쓰다 _ 2510

Dog's Thoughts

So many humans in this world,
strutting around, full of themselves.

One face on the outside,
another hidden deep inside—
greed and hypocrisy wrapped neatly in polite smiles.

When we're happy, we wag our tails.
When the feeling comes, we just go.

Isn't that better— the honesty of it?
At least we don't pretend.
At least we don't fake.

Written from a dog's point of view— watching a dog lift one leg on a neighborhood bench, doing its business without shame, and suddenly thinking: maybe this is the most honest dog's voice left in the world.

겨울 준비

청명한 들녘 누우런 알곡 떨어지면
곧 새하얀 눈 덮인 겨울이 오겠지요

덥다 더워 아 덥다
짜증일랑 좀 밀어두고

곧 닥칠 겨울 추위 생각하며
슬슬

장롱 속 깊은 곳 겨울 옷 몇 가지
털고 개키고 손봐야겠습니다

더위를 이기는 방법이 뭐 없을까?- 문득 떠오른 추운 겨울 생각을 옮기다 _
2408

Preparing for Winter

When the clear fields let their yellow grain fall,
winter will soon arrive, covered in clean white snow.

So hot—
too hot,
ah, this heat.
I'll push the irritation aside for now.

Thinking of the cold that's surely coming,
slowly—
gently—

I should take out a few winter clothes
from the depths of the closet,
shake them free, fold them again, set them in order.

Looking for a way to endure the heat—
and suddenly, finding myself thinking of winter.

공항 라운지

여행의 시작
공항 라운지

설렘의 퍼즐
공항 라운지

여행의 마침
공항 라운지

아쉬움의 정리
공항 라운지

Airport Lounge

The beginning of a journey—
the airport lounge.

A puzzle of anticipation—
the airport lounge.

The end of a journey—
the airport lounge.

Sorting through what lingers behind—
the airport lounge.

Written while sitting in the newly renewed lounge at Kansai International Airport, Osaka.

국어시간

국어시간이다 수업 들으러 와
선생님이 외친다

어라?
기역 니은 디귿은 간데없고

수학도 아니고 영어도 아닌
선생님의 허탄虛誕한 허세虛勢뿐

발라암Balaam 당나귀를 끌어와야 하나?

가르침 없는 교실엔 공허한 메아리만 가득
이리저리 우왕좌왕 길 잃은 양羊들만 가득

사무치게 그리워진다
초심初心의 국어시간

푸른 초원이 그리운 양羊의 입장에서 불편한 마음을 기록으로 남기다 _ 2303

Korean Language Class

It's Korean class—

come in and take your seats, the teacher calls out.

But wait.

Where did gi-yeok, ni-eun, di-geut go?

Not math. Not English.

Only the teacher's hollow words,

empty claims, loud with self-importance.

Do we need to bring in

Balaam's donkey to make the truth speak?

A classroom without teaching fills only with echoes—

sheep wandering in circles,

lost, with no pasture in sight.

I ache for it now,

deeply—

the Korean class of first intentions.

Written from the heart of a sheep longing for green fields—
leaving behind a record of quiet discomfort.

그곳

그리운 정감에 다시 찾은 그곳
깔끔히 단장한 기성복 같은 모습

나에게는 당황함이지만
너에게는 편리함이겠지

그 자리에 있던 기억 속 그 모습들
다시 찾을 때마다 하나둘 사라지니

서운한 마음
그리운 마음

가슴 깊은 속앓이 추억 붙잡는 이
말릴 수도 없고 되돌릴 수도 없고

There

I returned *there,*

drawn back by a familiar warmth.

Now it stands like ready-to-wear clothes—

clean, neatly dressed.

It unsettles me,

though for you it must be convenient.

The faces, the scenes that once lived in that place—

each time I return, they disappear, one by one.

A quiet disappointment.

A deeper longing.

Those who cling to memories,

holding them close in silent ache

no one can stop them,

no one can turn time back.

내 마음 안식처 이곳마저 변하니
이제 애써 찾아갈 그곳은 어딘가

그러나 쏟아지는 빗줄기 속
그곳엔 아직 따스함이 있다

Even this place,

once a refuge in my heart, has changed.

So now I ask myself—

where is the *there*

I would still make the effort to find?

And yet,

beneath the pouring rain,

there is still warmth

in *there*.

Saigon— a place that once carried the tenderness of childhood. Time moves on and convenience follows. Perhaps that, too, is part of being human.

그리움

도쿄 한복판
빌딩 숲을 거닐다

불현듯 엄마 생각
하늘을 바라보니

까마귀 한 마리
공중에 떠 날아간다

엄마는
하늘에 계신가 보다

안쓰러운 마음에
짠한 마음에

오늘도 아들 위로해 주려
하늘에서 내려다보시나 보다

일본 도쿄 출장 길 먼저 가신 어머니 생각에… _ 2304

Longing

In the heart of Tokyo,
walking through a forest of buildings,

Suddenly, I think of my mother.
I lift my eyes to the sky—

A single crow rises,
floating through the air.

My mother
must be in the sky.

With a tender ache,
with a quiet sorrow,

Perhaps today as well
she looks down from above,
trying to comfort her son.

Written on a business trip to Tokyo, thinking of my mother who passed away ahead of me.

금문교 2

흐르는 강물처럼 사랑도 흘러간다
어느 시인의 노래처럼

바람도 지나고 구름도 떠가듯
우리의 사랑도 흘러간다 금문교 다리 아래로

이 바람은 어디서 왔을까
저 구름은 또 어디서 왔을까

검푸른 바닷속 끝 모를 그 깊은 곳에도
우리의 사랑은 흘러간다 또다른 세계로

바람에 실려 물보라에 젖어
그렇게 흘러간다 의식 밖으로

반평생 함께 걸어온
애틋한 우리 사랑이여

해무海霧 짙게 깔린 금문교를 아내와 함께 걸어서 건너가며… _ 2301

The Golden Gate Bridge II

Like a flowing river,

love, too, moves on—

as in some poet's song.

As wind passes, as clouds drift away,

our love flows on, beneath the Golden Gate Bridge.

Where did this wind come from?

Where did those clouds come from?

Even into the unfathomable depths of the dark blue sea,

our love keeps flowing—

into another world.

Carried by the wind, soaked by ocean spray,

it drifts on, beyond consciousness.

O our love—

tender and enduring—

that has walked together for half a lifetime.

Written while walking across the Golden Gate Bridge with my wife, wrapped in thick sea fog.

기억 속의 얼굴

삶의 흔적 깊게 파인 친구들 얼굴에서
무심한 세월은 시위 떠난 화살과 같은가

쏜살같이 흘러간 젊음이라지만
다음 만남엔 또 어떤 모습일까

어느덧 사십여 년 지기 친구들
청순한 기억 속의 그 얼굴들

흐르는 눈물에 실어 보낸다
수다 뒤에 숨긴 애틋함 달래며

기억 속의 얼굴

첫 직장 동료 모임 후기 _ 2304

Faces in My Memory

In the faces of friends,
etched deeply with the marks of life,
has careless time
become an arrow loosed from its bow?

Youth may have rushed past like a sudden flight,
yet when we meet again,
what faces will we bring?

Friends of nearly forty years—
those faces once pure in memory.

I send them off on the flow of quiet tears,
soothing the tenderness hidden behind our chatter.

Written after a gathering with colleagues from my first workplace.

길을 걷다가

눈이 아직 떠지니
이름 모를 들꽃도 보고요

코도 아직 숨쉬니
싱그런 바람 내음도 맡고요

귀가 아직 밝으니
새소리 냇물 소리 좋고요

입도 아직 열리니
즐겁게 이야기할 수 있고요

뇌 또한 아직은 활동하니
생각을 글로 쓸 수 있고요

무엇보다 이런 즐거움 주는
짱짱한 무릎에 감사하네요

어느 날 동네 산책하다가 감사한 마음으로 적다 _ 2507

While Walking Down the Street

My eyes are still open,
so I can see
wildflowers I don't even know by name.

My nose still breathes,
so I can catch
the fresh scent of the passing breeze.

My ears are still clear,
so I can reach
the birdsong and the sound of running water.

My mouth still opens,
so I can talk,
and laugh, and share a moment.

My mind, too,
is still at work,
so thoughts can turn into words.

And above all, I'm grateful
for these strong, steady knees
that make all this possible.

While Walking Down the Street

Written with gratitude while walking through the neighborhood one day.

나이아가라 폭포

나이 좀 들어
다시 찾은 폭포 나이아가라

어마무시 쏟아지는 물 더미
천둥 같은 굉음

예전과 같은 듯
그전과 다른 듯

아름다운 무지개
폭포수에 걸렸다

무섭게 내리꽂는
물의 향연饗宴 바라보며

순응順應을 배운다
떨어져야 또 흐름이 있음을

거스름 없이 흘러 흘러
본향本鄕에 이를 수 있음을

30여 년만에 다시 찾아간 나이아가라 폭포를 보면서 느낀 소회所懷 _ 2309

Niagara Falls

Older now,
Niagara Falls, visited once again.

A massive weight of water pouring down—
a thunderous roar.

It feels the same,
yet not the same.

A beautiful rainbow
hangs in the falling water.

Watching this fierce descent,
this celebration of water,

I learn surrender.
Only by falling does the flow continue.

Without resistance, flowing and flowing,
we may finally reach our true home.

Written while standing before Niagara Falls again, after more than thirty years— reflecting on what time has taught me.

낙서 落書

길 위에 써 내려간
갈팡질팡 나의 낙서

시작은 있으나
끝은 모르는

발로 손으로
마음으로 오늘도

걸으며 쓰는 낙서
하늘로 이어지네

Scribble

A scribble I write along the road—
my own back and forth.

There is a beginning,
but no ending I can see.

With my feet,
with my hands,
with my heart—
today as well.

A scribble written while walking,
rising, until it reaches the sky.

Written as the title of my grandfather's notebook— *"Back and Forth"* came back to me.

낮아짐

주 앞에서 낮추어라
그리하면 주께서 너희를 높이시리라

겸손하여라
때가 되면 너희를 높이시리라

낮아짐으로 높아지는 매력
생각만 해도 기뻐지는 사람

나도 그런 사람이 되도록
기도하고 또 기도하여라

기쁨과 감사가 넘치는 삶으로
우리를 인도하리라

약 4:10, 벧전 5:6 묵상 _ 2308

Lowered

Humble yourself before the Lord,
and He will lift you up.

Be humble—
in due time,
He will raise you.

There is a grace in being lowered,
a beauty that rises from humility—
a person who brings joy even at the thought of them.

Let me become such a person.
I pray for it,
and pray again.

He will lead us into a life
overflowing with joy and gratitude.

A reflection on James 4:10 and 1 Peter 5:6.

내 마음의 수채화

그림을 그린다 물감 듬뿍 묻혀
붓 꼬리 가는 대로 터치를 한다

가늘게 때론 굵게
걸어온 여정대로

추억을 채운다
열정을 태운다

파아란 색으로
빠알간 색으로

손 끝에 묻어난
한 폭의 그림이

삶의 선물이려니 은혜의 번짐이려니
누군가와 마주할 소박한 사랑이려니

나의 두 번째 책 제목 『내 마음의 수채화』를 생각하며 적다. 세 번째는 뭐라
고 지을까? _ 2301

Watercolor of My Heart

I paint—

loading the brush with generous color,

letting the tip wander where it will.

Sometimes thin,

sometimes bold,

just like the road I have walked.

I fill it with memories.

I burn it with passion.

With deep blues.

With vivid reds.

At my fingertips,

a single painting takes shape.

Perhaps it is a gift of life.

Perhaps the spreading of grace.

Perhaps a simple love,

waiting to meet someone else.

Written while reflecting on the title of my second book, *Watercolor of My Heart*— and wondering what the third one might be called.

단골 식당

아내와 외식하러 찾아간 어느 날
동네 단골 식당이 문을 닫았다

기나긴 코로나로 어려운 탓인지
그 깊은 속내는 알 수 없지만

문이 잠긴 식당 물끄러미 바라보며
진한 아쉬움에 이리저리 둘러본다

불은 꺼져 있고 의자와 탁자는 온데간데없고
잡동사니 몇 가지 그저 바닥에 뒹굴고 있다

그래도

아내와의 웃음이 묻어 있는
사랑하는 이웃과의 추억이 서려 있는

My Favorite Restaurant

One evening,
my wife and I went out to eat—
and found our neighborhood favorite closed.

Perhaps the long years of COVID
made it too hard to go on.
I don't know the deeper reasons.

Standing there, staring at the locked door,
I linger—
heavy with regret, looking around.

The lights are off.
The chairs and tables are gone.
Only a few forgotten things lie scattered on the floor.

Still—

this place holds the laughter I shared with my wife,
the memories layered with neighbors I loved.

그래

이 식당은 나에게 행복인 거다
즐거운 기억으로 남아있는 거다

깜깜한 식당 문 앞 이리저리 서성이다가
굳게 닫힌 동네 단골식당 잠긴 문을 뒤로하고

아쉬움 가득 돌아서는 발걸음
애틋함으로 잔잔하게 물드는 내 가슴

Yes.

For me,
this restaurant was happiness.
It remains a joyful memory.

I pace for a moment before the darkened door,
then turn away
from the firmly closed entrance of our familiar place.

My steps leave slowly,
full of longing—
and my heart,
quietly,
fills with tenderness.

Written while standing before the locked door of a favorite neighborhood restaurant, on our way out to dinner.

달

새벽 하늘 언뜻
고개 들어 올려다보니

구름 한 점 없이
파아란 하늘에

점점 박힌 별과 하얀 달 하나
닿을 듯 말 듯 걸려 있구나

하늘 공중에 어떻게
저리 이쁘게 떠 있을까

하늘 푸르름에 긴장이 녹고
하얀 달 하나에 마음이 녹고

초겨울 새벽 하늘을 올려다보니 하얀 달 하나 청아하게 걸려 있구나! _ 2312

Moon

At dawn, almost without thinking,
I lift my head and look up.

Not a single cloud—
only a deep blue sky.

Stars pinned like dots, and one white moon,
hanging there, just out of reach.

How does it float so beautifully,
suspended in the open sky?

The blueness above loosens the tension in me,
and that single white moon melts my heart.

Written while gazing at the early winter dawn—
a single white moon, clear and pure, hanging in the sky.

땀

무더운 어느 여름날 길을 걷노라니
가로수 그늘 사이에서도 땀이 흐른다

머리카락 사이사이 송알송알 솟은 땀이
목덜미를 타고 내려 등줄기 적시고

발바닥까지 젖어온다
온 몸을 적신다

땀이 남은 건강함 젖은 몸이 감사하다
더위에 땀 흘리는 당연함이 감사하다

그 가운데 시원한 바람 한 줄기
참 감사하다 그 분의 손길이

Sweat

On a scorching summer day, walking down the street,
sweat still runs even in the shade of roadside trees.

Between strands of my hair, beads of sweat rise,
roll down my neck, soak my back—

all the way to the soles of my feet.
My whole body,
wet.

I'm grateful
for this body still healthy enough to sweat.
Grateful
that sweating in the heat is still something natural.

And in the middle of it all,
one cool line of breeze—
how grateful I am.
The touch of His hand.

Written while walking through the intense heat of midsummer, grateful even
for sweat streaming down.

도쿄 야경 바라보며

일본 출장 길 마지막 날 찾아간
호텔 꼭대기층 어느 레스토랑

와인 한 잔에 스시 몇 점 시키자니
저 멀리 도쿄타워 불이 들어온다

어둠을 밀어내고 아침이 오듯
땅거미 지자마자 불 켜지는 도시

새벽 햇살 기다림 참지 못하여
어두운 밤 사이사이 불을 밝힌다

나는 빛을 좋아하나 보다
어둠을 밀어내는 밝음이

Looking at the Night View of Tokyo

On the last night of a business trip to Japan,
I find myself
in a restaurant at the top floor of a hotel.

A glass of wine, a few pieces of sushi—
and far away,
Tokyo Tower lights up.

As morning pushes the darkness aside,
so this city,
the moment dusk arrives, turns on its lights.

Unable to wait for the first light of dawn,
it brightens the spaces between the dark.

I think I like light.
The brightness that drives the darkness back.

빛의 도쿄 이 야경이 좋은 것은
어둠이 싫은 게다 빛이 좋은 게다

하나 둘 밝아지는 빌딩 숲 등불
빛이 있으라 하니 빛이 있구나

It's so nice
this glowing Tokyo night—
It's not that I like the dark.
It's that I love the light.

One by one,
lamps rise in a forest of buildings.

Let there be light,
and there is light.

독일 소도시, 그 매력에 빠지다

올드 타운 골목길 중세의 돌담
뾰족한 첨탑 아래 우뚝 선 교회

고즈넉함 간직한 고요 속 소요
보듬고 느끼고 어루만지고

루터의 기도 소리
괴테의 슬픈 노래

돌담 사이사이 철학과
베토벤의 운명까지도

묻고 답하며 걷고 또 걷네
독일 소도시 그 매력에 빠져

크리스마스 즈음 독일의 몇몇 소도시를 여행하며 느낀 생각을 적다 _ 2501

A Small Town in Germany
— Falling for Its Charm

65

Stone walls of the Middle Ages along Old Town alleys,
a church standing tall beneath a pointed spire.

A quiet calm, a gentle wandering in stillness—
holding it, feeling it, letting it rest in my hands.

Luther's prayers echo softly,
Goethe's sorrowful songs linger in the air.

Between the stones, philosophy breathes,
and even Beethoven's Fate seems to pass by.

Asking and answering,
walking and walking again,
I find myself falling
for the charm of a small German town.

Written while traveling through several small towns in Germany around Christmastime.

등목背沐

푹푹찌는 무더위 7월 어느 날
주체할 수 없이 줄줄 흐르는 땀

셔츠 바지 훌훌 벗어 던지고
수돗물 샤워에 몸을 맡긴다

마중물 한 바가지 부어넣고
지하수 열심히 펌프질하여

물을 끼얹고 문지르며
시원하냐 어머니 음성

차가운 물 그 거칠한 손바닥
어디서 다시 느낄 수 있을까

무지 더운 여름날 샤워하다 떠오른 어머니의 등목背沐 그리고 그 음성 _
2507

Pouring Water Over My Back

On a sweltering day in July, the heat pressing hard,

sweat pouring down beyond control.

I peel off my shirt and pants,

let my body lean into the rush of tap water.

One bucket first— the priming splash,

then the pump works hard,

drawing cold water up from below.

Water poured, hands rubbing—

Is it cool enough?

my mother's voice.

That cold water,

those rough palms—

where could I ever feel them again?

Written on a brutally hot summer day, while showering— suddenly remembering my mother pouring water over my back, and the sound of her voice.

렉시오 디비나 콘티누아

책을 읽자
끊임없이 렉시오LECTIO 하자

어쩌다가 잠깐 하는 운동
근력이 생기는가?

수적천석水滴穿石
끊임없이 떨어지는 물방울이 돌을 뚫는 법

콘티누아CONTINUA 하자
메마른 영혼을 위해

읽고 묵상默想하고
기도하고 관상觀想하고

하나님 말씀으로
일상日常을 채우자

렉시오 디비나 콘티누아LECTIO DIVINA CONTINUA

김병삼 목사의 새벽말씀을 듣고 느낌을 적다 _ 2401

Lectio Divina Continua

Let us read.
Let us practice *lectio*—
without ceasing.

Can strength be built
from exercise done only once in a while?

Drop by drop,
water pierces stone.

So let us continue—
continua—
for our thirsty souls.

Read. Meditate.
Pray. Contemplate.

Let the Word of God
fill our ordinary days.

Lectio Divina Continua.

Written after listening to an early-morning message of Pastor Kim
Byung-sam— a quiet resolve set down in words.

로보킹

우리 집 구석구석 깨끗하게 책임지는
군말 없이 명령대로 말 잘 듣는 로보킹

어느 날 외출하여 돌아와 보니
방구석에 덩그러니 처박혀 있다

이거 왜 이러시나
시키지도 않았는데

이 친구도 함께 늙어가나 보다
치매인가 세월의 무게 짓눌려

괜한 안쓰러움에 가만히 들어올려
제자리인 충전기에 올려놓는다

Roboking

The one who keeps every corner of our home clean,
never complains,
follows commands—
Roboking.

One day I come home,
and there it is,
abandoned in a corner of the room.

What's going on with you?
I didn't even tell you to go or to stop.

Maybe this one, too,
is growing old with me.
Is it memory loss,
or just the weight of time?

With a needless tenderness,
I quietly lift it up and place it back
where it belongs—
on the charging dock.

충전을 시작합니다
주인님 사랑합니다

말은 곧잘 하는데 어이할거나
버리자니 짠하고 쓰자니 으음

<hr>

우리 집에 오래된 로봇 청소기 하나— 시도 때도 없이 제멋대로 다니는 모습
을 보며 인간의 늙음이 떠올라 적다 _ 2510

Charging has started.
Master, I love you.

It talks so well—

what am I supposed to do with that?

Throw it away, and it feels cruel.

Keep using it, and—

well⋯ hmm.

Written while watching an old robot vacuum at home—
wandering off on its own, again—
and again and suddenly thinking of how humans, too, grow old.

루틴

때가 되면 밥을 먹고
때가 되면 잠을 자고

눈을 뜨면 기도하고
책을 읽고 멍 때리고

낮에는 일을 하고
마치면 가정으로

루틴은 일상이려니
커다란 굴레려니

세상에 온 것도
흙으로 돌아감도

행복은 그 안에 있으려니

굴레 너머 아닌
지금 여기에

새벽녘 책을 읽다가 날마다 반복되는 일상에 웃음짓다 _ 2505

Routine

When it's time, I eat.
When it's time, I sleep.

I open my eyes—
pray, read,
stare into nothing for a while.

By day, I work.
When it's done, I return home.

Routine—
maybe just daily life,
maybe a wide, enclosing circle.

Coming into this world,
returning to dust—

perhaps happiness lives inside it.

Not beyond the circle,
but right here.
Right now.

Written at dawn, smiling to myself while reading a book and thinking about
the days that repeat.

만남

모처럼인데도
마치

어제인 듯 반가움은
시간의 간극 지우고

주 안에서 하나 됨은
모든 걸 녹이고 녹여

유쾌한 수다로
즐거운 웃음으로

울컥 서러움도
따뜻한 사랑 안에

주거니 받거니
성령의 기운

마음은 벌써
다음 만남으로

경건한 자매들과의 만남 후기 _ 2504

Seeing

It's been a while—
and yet,
it feels like yesterday.

The joy erases
the distance of time.

Being one in the Lord
melts everything, again and again.

With cheerful chatter,
with easy laughter—

even the sudden ache
finds its way into warm love.

Giving and receiving,
back and forth—
the breath of the Spirit.

And already,
my heart is leaning
toward our next meeting.

Written after a gathering with devoted sisters in faith.

바람

바람이 분다

바람에 바람을 실어 보낸다

사랑도 싣고

그리움도 싣고

먼 곳에도 바람은 불겠지

그곳에서도

바람에 실린 바람을 느끼겠지

오늘도

바람이 분다

싱그러운 바람결 속에 불현듯 호주에 사는 사랑하는 딸 혜영이가 생각나 한 줄 적다 _ 2507

Wind and Wish

The wind blows.

I send my wishes on the wind.

I send my love.

I send my longing.

The wind must be blowing
far away, too.

And there—
you must be feeling it,
the wish carried by the wind.

Today,
once again,

the wind blows.

Written when a fresh breeze passed— and suddenly I thought of my beloved daughter, Hyeyoung, living far away in Australia.

벚꽃처럼

시련과 환난도
기쁨으로 받으면

아무리 추워도
기어이 봄은 오리

물올라 피어나는
화사한 벚꽃처럼

푸릇푸릇 터지는
봄의 소리 들으리

벚꽃처럼

동네 천변에 핀 벚꽃을 바라보다가 _ 2403

Like Cherry Blossoms

If trials and hardships
are received with joy,

no matter how cold it is,
spring will surely come.

Like cherry blossoms,
rising with sap,
bursting into bloom—

we will hear the sound of spring,
fresh and green,
breaking open.

Written while gazing at cherry blossoms in bloom along the neighborhood stream

보리굴비

커다란 보리굴비 한 마리 저녁 밥상에 올랐다
맛난 보리굴비 한 점 크게 베어먹다 문득

요 녀석은 어떤 생生을 살았을까
문득 궁금해진다

그저 짭쪼롬 바닷물과 해초의 맛에 취해
무념無念으로 살점만 불려 왔을까

무얼 바라 그토록 열심 내어 헤엄쳤을까
이 밥상 위 누울 줄도 모른 채

A Dried Barley Croaker

A large dried croaker
is placed on the dinner table.
I take a generous bite—
salty, rich—
and suddenly,

I wonder.
What kind of life did this one live?

Drunk only on briny seawater and seaweed,
did it grow its flesh
without thought,
without desire?

What was it chasing,
swimming so earnestly,
never knowing it would end up lying on this table?

보리굴비 한 마리 감사히 먹다가
겹쳐지고 대비되는

물고기의 생生
나의 인생人生

저녁 밥상에 올라온 보리굴비 한 마리를 먹다가 잡생각이 떠올라 기록하다 _ 2304

As I finish this fish
with gratitude,
two lives overlap,
then stand apart—

the life of a fish,
and the life of my own.

Written when stray thoughts arose while eating a dried barley croaker at the dinner table.

본향本鄕

봄비와 함께한 서울 나들이
촉촉한 정으로 만남을 갖고

남쪽으로 남쪽으로 내려가는 길
쇳덩어리 물결에 답답은 해도

본향本鄕에 이르면
또 아쉬움 있으리

온 몸으로 부대낀
카미노Camino 추억에

지인과의 분당 회동 후 집으로 내려 오는 길— 많은 차들로 길이 막힌 고속도
로 위 버스 안에서 지루함을 달래며 적다 _ 2405

The Original Hometown

A spring rain accompanies

a day out in Seoul—

meetings warmed by gentle affection.

Heading south,

farther and farther south,

the road feels tight,

a tide of steel and engines.

Yet when I reach my original hometown,

there will be another kind of longing—

memories of the Camino,

pressed into me

with my whole body.

Written on the way home after meeting an acquaintance in Bundang— on a crowded highway bus, passing time and easing the boredom.

봄

눈앞에 봄이 보이기 시작한다
아니 보이기 시작하니 봄인가

누우런 잔디 사이 새싹 보이고
잿빛 가지 사이 꽃망울 보이고

냉기 품은 봄비 빗방울 사이로
따스한 기운 스멀스멀 보인다

봄을 시샘하는 눈발 속에도
흙먼지 굴리는 바람 속에도

파룻한 이파리 보이기 시작한다
화사한 꽃잎이 보이기 시작한다

봄은 기어이 오고야 만다
눈을 감아도 기어이 온다

봄을 시샘하듯 내리는 눈 바라보며 _ 2503

Spring

Spring begins to appear before my eyes—
or perhaps,
because it appears, it is already spring.

Between yellowed grass,
new shoots show themselves.
Between ashen branches,
flower buds begin to form.

Through cold drops of spring rain,
a gentle warmth slowly rises.

Even in snowflakes jealous of spring,
even in winds kicking up dust,

fresh green leaves begin to appear.
Bright petals begin to appear.

Spring will come, inevitably.
Even if I close my eyes, it comes all the same.

Written while watching snow fall, as if begrudging the arrival of spring.

부끄러움

부끄러움
그것은 망신이 아니라 겸손이다

부끄러움
그것은 수치가 아니라 떳떳함이다

부끄러움
그것은 잘못된 생각의 깨달음이다

부끄러움
그것을 인정하고 나를 다시 세우자

김병삼 목사의 '하나님의 시선'을 듣고(마 10:27) _ 2502

Shame

Shame—

it is not disgrace,

but humility.

Shame—

it is not humiliation,

but integrity.

Shame—

it is the moment

wrong thinking is awakened.

Shame—

let us acknowledge it,

and stand ourselves up again.

Written after listening to Pastor Kim Byung-sam's *God's Perspective*, reflecting on Matthew 10:27.

비아 돌로로사

글로만 읽던 길 귀로만 듣던 길
고통의 그 길 십자가의 길

나도 따라 걸어가네
비아 돌로로사Via Dolorosa

우리들 죄의 멍에 짊어지고
피 흘리며 끌려가신 그 길을

찔림의 아픔 조롱의 치욕
시공간 넘어 함께하며

두 눈 가득 고인 눈물 주르륵
걷는 내내 울었다

십자가에 매달린 죽음이 아니라
우리 등을 토닥여주는 살아 계심으로

Via Dolorosa

A road I once knew only through words,
a road I had heard only with my ears—
the road of suffering,
the road of the cross.

Now I walk it myself,
Via Dolorosa.

The road where He carried
the weight of our sins,
bled, and was dragged forward.

The piercing pain,
the shame of mockery—
crossing time and space,
I walk with Him.

Tears fill my eyes,
spill over—
I cried the entire way.

Not a death hanging on a cross,
but a living presence
patting our backs, telling us to go on.

나를 위하여 울지 말고
너희와 너희 자녀를 위하여 울라 하신

그 말씀 은혜 되어 눈물
성령의 위로하심에 또 눈물

비아 돌로로사 걸음걸음 그 길 위에
이마와 두 손 펼쳐 통곡의 벽 기대어

통곡하는 가운데 어디선가 들리는 음성
심령이 가난한 자는 복을 받을지니

눈물 떨구며 걸어가네
예루살렘 비아 돌로로사

성령이 함께한 성지 여행길— 이스라엘 벤구리온 공항(the Ben Gurion Airport)에
서 적다 _ 2302

Do not weep for me,
but for yourselves
and for your children.

Those words turn into grace,
and again—
tears at the consolation of the Holy Sprit.

Along each step of Via Dolorosa,
I press my forehead, spread my hands,
and lean against the Wailing Wall.

In the midst of my sobbing,
a voice is heard from somewhere—
Blessed are the poor in spirit.

Dropping tears as I walk,
I move forward
along Via Dolorosa, Jerusalem.

Written during a Holy Land pilgrimage, with the Holy Spirit near—
set down at Ben Gurion Airport, Israel.

Chapter 1

작은 글 모음

Ⅱ 사 - 아

ㅐ

사

ㅡ

아

사랑

하나님은 사랑이시다
그 사랑으로 지음 받은 인간

살아있음은
존재의 의미는

사랑이 없으면
아무 것도 아니다

다시 돌아가자
진실된 사랑으로

바로잡자 잘못된 것들을
가 없는 그 크신 사랑으로

대속의 피 짙게 묻은
그 사랑의 십자가로

Love

God is love.

And humanity was created from that love.

To be alive—

the meaning of our being—

Without love,

we are nothing.

Let us return,

back to love that is true.

Let us set right what has gone wrong,

with that great love that lacks nothing.

By the cross of love,

deeply stained with the blood of redemption.

Written while thinking deeply about the future and happiness of my beloved son.

사이공 1

오랜만에 다시 찾은 사이공
코로나 이후라 더 반가운 사이공

철없이 기세등등하던 시절
필라델피아 연수 길에 접한

뉴욕 브로드웨이 뮤지컬
*미스 사이공*의 추억

다 알아듣지 못한들 어떠랴
분위기에 흠뻑 취했던 기억이 새롭다

나에게 위안을 주는 사이공
아래를 보고 살라는 지혜를 주는 곳

Saigon I

Saigon—
returning after a long while.
Even more welcome after the years of COVID.

Back when I was young,
reckless, full of swagger,
on a training trip to Philadelphia,

I met Saigon through *Miss Saigon*,
a Broadway musical in New York.

I didn't understand every word—
so what?
I remember being swept up
by the mood, the feeling.

Saigon comforts me.
It teaches me to live looking downward,
to stay grounded.

쪼끄만 휴지 몇 봉지
길바닥에 깔아 놓고

코흘리개 아이 손잡고
농Nón 눌러쓴 채 돈을 구하는 여인

엄마는 작은 숯불 화덕 위
뭔가를 구워 내고

딸아이는 조막만한 손 벌려
손님 돈 받아 들어 비닐봉지에 담고

목욕탕 의자
삼삼오오 모여 앉아

사이공 진한 커피에
고수향 박하향 가득 음식에

A few small packs of tissues
spread on the pavement.

A woman, a sniffling child's hand in hers,
a conical hat pulled low, asking for coins.

A mother tending a tiny charcoal stove,
grilling something warm.

A little girl, palms no bigger than leaves,
receiving money, placing it carefully into a plastic bag.

Bathhouse stools,
people gathered in small clusters.

Strong Saigon coffee,
food rich with cilantro and mint.

바라만 봐도 위안이요 평안함 주는
이런 사이공이 나는 감사하다

부족해도 넉넉한 삶의 모습이
저절로 내려놓고 비우게 만드니

가끔은 일부러라도 와서 접하고픈
깨달음 주는 사이공이 나는 참 좋다

Even just watching—

I feel comforted, at peace.

For this Saigon,

I am grateful.

Lives that look lacking yet feel abundant—

they make me loosen my grip,

they make me empty myself.

Sometimes, I want to come here on purpose,

just to encounter it again.

This Saigon—

the one that gives me insight—

I truly love it.

Written while traveling in Saigon, recording the impressions that stayed with me.

사이공 2

사람 사는 냄새가 좋다
그들의 행복한 얼굴이 좋다

어릴 적 추억의 판박이가 좋다
아직은 남아있는 정감이 좋다

이곳으로 나를 이끄는
무더위마저도 손을 내미는

2% 부족한 어설픔조차
시크함으로 포장한 순진함마저

여기저기 솟구치는 젊음의 역동
여기오면 느끼는 살아있음이 좋다

사이공 뒷골목 젊음의 거리ㅡ 떠들썩한 펍(Pub)에서 젊은 베트남 친구와 큰
얼음 가득 채운 사이공 맥주를 시원하게 한 잔 하며 기록하다 _ 2503

Saigon II

I like the smell of people living their lives.

I like the happiness on their faces.

I like how it mirrors the memories of my childhood.

I like the warmth that still remains here.

Even the heavy heat

that draws me back to this place reaches out its hand.

Even the awkwardness,

that missing two percent—

even the innocence wrapped in cool indifference.

Youth bursting out everywhere,

energy rising from the streets—

when I'm here, I feel it:

I am alive.

Written in a back alley of Saigon, on a street alive with youth—
sharing a cold Saigon beer, packed with ice, with a young Vietnamese
friend in a lively pub.

삶은 계란

斷想 _ 2412

껍질을 깨고 벗겨내니
그제야 하얀 속살이 드러난다

이게 끝이 아니다
흰자 벗겨내야 노른자 보인다

껍데기는 가라
보여주기 위한 치장은 버려라

껍질 속 깊숙이 놓여 있는 노른자
노엘Noel을 통해 드러나는 사랑

위선의 가면을 벗어야 느낀다
사랑의 마음을 품어야 맛본다

온기 남은 삶은 계란 하나
사랑이 있고 부활이 있고

크리스마스 즈음 프랑크푸르트 어느 호텔에서 아침 식사를 하며 떠오른 단상
斷想 _ 2412

Boiled Egg

I crack the shell,

peel it away—

only then does the white flesh appear.

But this is not the end.

Peel away the white, and the yolk is revealed.

Let the shell go.

Discard the decorations meant only to be seen.

Deep inside the shell,

the yolk waits—

love revealed through Noel.

Only when the mask of hypocrisy is removed

can it be felt.

Only when the heart holds love

can it be tasted.

A single boiled egg, still warm—

within it, there is love,

and there is resurrection.

Written while having breakfast at a hotel in Frankfurt, around Christmastime—
a fleeting reflection set down in words.

삼겹살

아들
삼겹살 먹을래?

나이 지긋한 엄니가
전화를 한다

아뇨
걍 집에서 대충 먹을래요

엄니는 삼겹살이 먹고 싶었을까?
아들 얼굴이 보고 싶었을까?

엄니와 아들의 선문답에
아빠는 그저 실소失笑 뿐

집착하자니 우상
놓아주자니 애틋함

Grilled Pork Belly

Son,
do you want some pork belly?

An aging mother
calls on the phone.

No—
I'll just eat something simple at home.

Did she want pork belly?
Or did she want
to see her son's face?

In this riddle between mother and son,
the father can only let out a quiet chuckle.

Hold on too tight,
and it becomes an idol.
Let go,
and it turns into longing.

벗어날 수 없는 정情의 굴레에
죄 없는 삼겹살만 오늘도 그저

이리 치이고
저리 치이고

Caught in a bond of affection no one can escape,

the innocent pork belly,

once again today, gets pushed around—

this way,

and that.

Written while overhearing a phone call between my wife and our son.

산상 예배

갈릴리 호숫가 아름다움 서린
산상수훈 설파하신 팔복산에 올라

심령이 가난한 자는 복이 있나니 천국이 그들의 것임이요
여덟 가지 복을 곱씹어 본다

오병이어 모자이크 정원을 돌아
파아란 잔디밭 위 둘러 앉아서

성지투어 주일예배 아내와 둘이서
눈을 들어 산을 보니 찬송을 한다

팔각지붕 팔복교회 신비와 경건에 젖어
여호수와 축복받은 갈렙 이야기

Worship at the Church of the Beatitudes

Climbing the mount
by the beauty of the Sea of Galilee,
the hill where the Sermon on the Mount was proclaimed.

Blessed are the poor in spirit,
for theirs is the kingdom of heaven.
I linger over the eight blessings, one by one.

Walking through
the mosaic garden of the five loaves and two fish,
we sit together on the deep green grass.

A Sunday worship on pilgrimage—
my wife and I, side by side, singing,
I lift my eyes to the hills.

Under the octagonal roof of the Church of the Beatitudes,
soaked in mystery and reverence,
we hear of Joshua, and Caleb,
the one who received the blessing.

선교사 입술 통해 말씀 들으며
벅찬 감동으로 물드는 가슴

두세 사람이 내 이름으로 모인 곳에는
나도 그들 중에 있느니라 하신 것처럼

예배 가운데 흐르는 눈물 있으니
성령이 함께 하심이라

아멘

Through the lips of a Missionary,

the Word is spoken—

and my heart fills, to the brim.

For where two or three

are gathered in my name,

there am I among them.

As if to answer that promise,

tears flow

within the worship—

the Holy Spirit

is here.

Amen.

Written in reflection on Sunday worship at the Church of the Beatitudes in Galilee (Sermon text: Joshua 14:6–14).

샴페인

깔때 모양 와인 잔 타고 오르며
점점이 방울방울 깨어나는 샴페인

중력을 거슬러 치고 오르는 기세
누구도 막지 못하는 힘이 넘치네

개혁은 믿음 변화는 용기
꾹꾹 억눌렸던 가슴 터진다

FF공항 라운지에서 샴페인 잔 타고 오르는 아름다운 기포를 바라보며, 종교
개혁 시발점인 마르틴 루터의 비텐베르크 성교회를 방문한 느낌을 정리하다 _
2508

Champagne

Rising through a funnel-shaped glass,

champagne awakens—

bubble by bubble.

A surge climbing against gravity,

a force no one can hold back.

Reformation is faith.

Transformation is courage.

A chest long pressed down—

at last,

bursting open.

Written at an airport lounge, watching champagne bubbles rise— reflecting on a visit to Wittenberg, the birthplace of the Reformation, where Martin Luther once stood.

새벽에 내린 서리

사무실 밖 자동차에 서리가 앉았다
잎 떨어진 작달막한 나뭇가지에도

물감을 발라도 모자를 뒤집어써도
귓등 위 새하얀 서리 비집고 나온다

자연의 법칙은
겨울이 지나면 봄이 오건만

유한한 인생은
머리에 서리 앉으면 마감의 시작

갈무리 잘하고 하늘로 올라가자
이름 석 자 하나 깔끔히 남겨두고

초겨울 아침 사무실 밖 거닐다가 새벽에 내린 서리를 바라보며 적다 _ 2411

Early-Morning Frost

Frost has settled on the cars outside the office,
on the short, bare branches stripped of leaves.

No matter the dye,
no matter the hat pulled low,
white frost still pushes through above the ears.

The law of nature is simple—
after winter, spring comes.

But a finite life is different.
When frost settles on the head, the closing begins.

Let us gather things well,
and rise toward the sky—
leaving behind, clean and clear,
nothing more than a name of three simple letters.

Written while walking outside the office on an early winter morning,
watching frost left behind by dawn.

선善과 악惡

선善은

악惡을 이기지 못한다

이 세상에서는

Good and Evil

Good

does not overcome

evil.

Not

in this world.

Written while pausing in thought over a small collection of Schopenhauer's writings.

설날 1

새해 복 많이 받으세요
매년 반복되는 인사말

나이 칠십 가까우니
두근대는 마음도 무감각하다

어머니도 떠나고
아버지도 떠나고

딱히 오갈 데 없는 발길은
어머니 집으로 향한다

엄니
저 왔어요

공허한 메아리만
텅 빈 내 가슴에

까치라도 한 번
울어주면 좋으련만

새해 첫날 고향에 계시던 어머니 생각에 갈 곳 없는 나그네 한 줄 적다 _ 2301

Lunar New Year I

Happy New Year.

The same greeting, repeated every year.

Now, nearing seventy,

even the flutter of the heart has grown numb.

My mother is gone.

My father is gone.

With nowhere in particular to go,

my steps turn toward my mother's house.

Mom—

I'm here.

Only an empty echo

returns, into the hollow of my chest.

If only a magpie would cry out once,

at least once.

Written on the first day of the Lunar New Year, as a wanderer with
nowhere to go, thinking of my mother who once waited in my hometown.

설날 2

책상 위 달력 마지막 장 넘기면
어김없이 눈 앞에 다가오는 설날

까치까치 설날은 어저께고요
우리우리 설날은 오늘이라는데

설렘은 나이에 반비례하나
갈라터진 마음 논바닥처럼

지인의 부고 한 장 받아들고 보니
누군가엔 슬픈 날이기도 하리라

자식들 찾아오려니 위안 삼아
저으기 설렘을 가장해 본다

유난히 긴 2025 설날 연휴를 보내는 중, 지인으로부터 갑자기 날아온 부고
소식에 _ 2501

Lunar New Year II

When I turn the last page of the desk calendar,
the Lunar New Year arrives again, right on time.

Magpie, magpie,
yesterday was your New Year—
our New Year is today, they say.

But excitement seems to fade as age increases,
like cracked rice fields in a long drought.

Holding a single obituary notice,
I realize—
for someone, today is also a day of sorrow.

Still, I tell myself my children will come to visit,
and I try—
just a little—
to pretend in borrowed excitement.

Written during an unusually long Lunar New Year holiday in 2025,
after the sudden news of a friend's passing.

성지 여행

인생 버킷 리스트 고대하던 성지 여행
이천 년 아니 그 이상의 시간을 뛰어넘어

비아 돌로로사Via Dolorosa 고난의 길 돌아
통곡의 벽 기대어 회한의 눈물 뿌린다

정교회 지하 말구유 베들레헴 별
무릎 꿇어 매만지며 낮은 곳으로

목자들의 들판교회 천사들과 함께
노엘Noel 노엘을 목청껏 찬송한다

산상수훈 설파하신 갈릴리 팔복교회
여덟 가지 복 되새기며 산상예배 드리고

A Trip to the Hly Land

A lifelong bucket list,
a long-awaited pilgrimage—
leaping across two thousand years,
no—
far more than that.

I walk the Via Dolorosa, the road of suffering,
lean against the Wailing Wall,
and scatter tears of regret.

Beneath the Orthodox Church, at Bethlehem's manger star,
I kneel, touch it with my hands,
learning the way of low places.

At the Shepherds' Field Church, with angels near,
I lift my voice—
Noel, Noel—
singing aloud.

At the Church of the Beatitudes in Galilee,
where the Sermon on the Mount was spoken,
I turn over the eight blessings and offer worship on the hill.

요단강 세례 터 두 손 담가 회개하니
가서 다시는 죄를 짓지 말고 평안히 가라

세례 요한 말씀이 들리지 않는가?

가나 혼인잔치 첫 기적을 함께하며
시온산 마가의 다락방 마지막 성만찬도

감람산 자락 겟세마네 만국교회
피눈물로 기도하던 그 모습과 겹친다

돌에 맞아 순교한 스데반의 영혼
사도 바울은 무슨 생각을 하는가?

At the Jordan River Baptismal site,

I dip both hands,

repent—

Go, and sin no more.

Go in peace.

Do you not hear the voice of John the Baptist?

At Cana,

sharing the first miracle of the wedding feast,

then to Mount Zion,

the Upper Room of Mark, the Last Supper.

At Gethsemane,

the Church of All Nations

on the slope of the Mount of Olives—

His prayer, like drops of blood, overlaps with mine.

The soul of Stephen,

stoned to death—

what was Paul thinking then?

다윗의 지혜 깃든 시온산
아브라함 순종 서린 성전산
예언대로 메시아 오신 감람산
솔로몬 첩들의 여러 우상 멸망산

왼편부터 천천히 고개 끄덕이며

사해 서쪽 소돔산에 굳어버린 롯의 아내
고모라 유황 불 바라보며 후회하겠지

겨자씨 돌갓 꽃과 언약괘 싯딤Shittim 나무
샤론의 꽃 아네모네 아름다움에 취한 채

문명의 혜택 케이블카로
시험산The Mt Temptation 꼭대기 산상에 올라
사탄Satan의 유혹에 나는 어떠한가

Mount Zion, bearing David's wisdom.
The Temple Mount, marked by Abraham's obedience.
The Mount of Olives, where the Messiah came, as foretold.
The Mount of Destruction, where Solomon's idols fell.

From left to right, I nod slowly.

Lot's wife, hardened into salt
on Mount Sodom, west of the Dead Sea—
did she regret it,
looking back at sulfur and fire over Gomorrah?

Mustard seed and flowers,
the Shittim wood of the Ark of the Covenant,
the anemone—
the Rose of Sharon—
drunk on their beauty.

By the grace of modern convenience,
a cable car lifts me to the Mount of Temptation.
Before Satan's lure,
who am I?

종려나무 성읍 여리고Jerico 삭개오는
그 천한 돌무화과나무Sycamore에 올라
왜 그토록 간절하게 예수를 만나려 했을까

새 그릇에 소금을 담아 내게로 가져오라한
엘리사Elisha의 기적을 다시 바랐던 것일까?

하나님의 포도원 카르멜산 수도원 들러
하나님의 사람 엘리야를 만나고

탁 트인 수시타Susita 언덕에 올라
사반Shaphan 과 함께 갈릴리 호수 바라보니

천만 년 이어져온 그 대지 위
진홍색 붉은 석양 호수면에 부서진다

저 멀리 가나안 땅 바라보던 모세는
느보산 위에서 과연 무슨 생각을 하는가

In Jericho, the city of palms,
Zacchaeus climbed that low sycamore tree—
why was he so desperate to see Jesus?

Was it Elisha's miracle he longed for—
Bring me a new bowl with salt in it?

At Mount Carmel, God's vineyard,
I meet Elijah, the man of God.

Climbing the open hills of Susita,
with rock hyrax nearby,
I gaze upon the Sea of Galilee—

upon land ten million years old,
a crimson sunset shattering across the water.

Moses,
looking toward Canaan from afar—
what, I wonder,
was he thinking on Mount Nebo?

Written during a pilgrimage to Israel— with the Holy Spirit walking alongside.

세월무상 歲月無常

올해 몇인가

70 넘은
선배가 묻는다

66입니다

왜 이리
빨리 쫓아오나?

그러게요

60 넘으니
브레이크가 고장이네요

허 어
그거 참

Time Flies

How old are you now?

A senior, past seventy,
asks.

Sixty-six.

*Why are you catching up
so fast?*

I don't know.

After sixty,
the brakes seem broken.

*Huh—
well then.*

Written after a quiet conversation over a cup of tea with a senior.

솔로몬의 독백

눈도 침침하고
돋보기 없이는 글자 한 자 읽기도 힘들다

밥상머리 밥그릇 안
밥 알도 잘 안보인다

늙으면 죽어야 혀
옛 어른들의 독백이 생각나는 나이다

내가 벌써?

애써 부인해도 어쩔 수 없는 건 어쩔 수 없다
참으로 어리석은 게 인간인가 보다

똑똑하고 지혜로운 척은 혼자 다 하면서
눈 앞의 밥 알 하나도 제대로 보지 못한다

Solomon's Monologue

My eyes grow dim.
Without reading glasses,
I can barely make out a single letter.

Even at the dinner table,
inside my bowl,
the grains of rice refuse to come into focus.

When you grow old, you should die.
The muttering of the elders—
I remember it now.

Already?
Me?

No matter how hard I deny it,
what cannot be helped cannot be helped.
How foolish human beings are.

We pretend to be wise, pretend to be clever,
yet cannot clearly see a single grain of rice
right before us.

이런 우라질
악이 받친들 어쩔 건데?

그 분의 영역은 그 분에게 남겨두자
내가 넘보려 바둥대지 말자

서글픔은 분노를 분노는 짜증을
짜증은 체념에 이르노니

헛되고 헛된 것이
인생인가보다

Damn it—

even if anger rises,

what good does it do?

Let His realm

remain His.

Let me stop struggling to trespass there.

Sorrow becomes anger.

Anger turns into irritation.

Irritation settles into resignation.

Vanity of vanities—

perhaps this

is life.

Written while rubbing tired eyes, midway through a spoonful of dinner.
(Ecclesiastes 1:2)

스미노에 온천

온천에서 느낀 생각 _ 2411

붉은 와인 빛 노천탕 안에
지긋이 눈을 감고 몸을 맡긴다

탕 안 가장자리 백발의 노인 셋
작은 이야기로 피로를 털어낸다

온천을 즐기는 오사카 노인
나도 즐기는 일본의 온천

맑고 파아란 하늘 위 구름은 흘러가고
탕 위론 시나브로 물안개 피어오르고

천국이 어디인가 궁금해 말자
여기가 바로 거기 그 곳 아닌가

Suminoe Hot Spring

In an open-air bath, tinted the color of red wine,
I close my eyes and let my body drift.

At the edge of the pool,
three white-haired elders
shake off their fatigue with quiet talk.

Osaka elders enjoying the hot spring—
and I, too, enjoying Japan's waters.

Above,
a clear blue sky, clouds passing by.
Around the bath,
steam rises—
softly, little by little.

Don't ask where heaven is.
Isn't this place,
right here,
already there?

Written from thoughts that surfaced while soaking in a hot spring.

시인

시인은 시를 쓰는 사람인가?

인사를 하는 사람이다
안부를 묻는 사람이다
대화를 하는 사람이다

꽃하고도
나비하고도
돌멩이하고도

하물며 사람일까보냐

우리 모두 시인이 되자
사랑으로 가득한 세상 함께 만들자

지인이 시인이 되었다는 소식에 떠오른 생각을 적다 _ 2408

Poet

Is a poet
someone who writes poems?

A poet is someone
who greets,
who asks how you are,
who knows how to talk.

With flowers.
With butterflies.
With stones.

How much more so—
with people?

Let us all become poets.
Let us make, together,
a world filled with love.

Poet

Written after hearing that a dear acquaintance had become a poet.

아내에게 바치는 노래 2

우리 아내는 참 곱다

세월의 흐름에 순종하여
초겨울 풀잎 위 하아얀 서리처럼

희끗희끗 내려앉은
머리칼도 곱고

살짜기 입가에 웃음이 번진
잔잔하게 미소 띤 그 얼굴도 곱다

화려한 예쁨이 아닌
은은한 온화溫和 머금은

우리 아내는 참 곱다

가족 향한 사랑이나
이웃사촌에게나

섬기는 그 마음이 곱다
한결같은 그 마음이

A Song Dedicated to My Wife II

My wife is truly beautiful.

Yielding to the flow of time,
like white frost resting on grass in early winter—

even the silver strands settling into her hair
are beautiful.

The gentle smile
that softly spreads at the corner of her lips,
that calm, smiling face—
beautiful.

Not a showy beauty,
but one that holds a quiet warmth.

My wife is truly beautiful.

In her love for family,
in her kindness toward neighbors—

the heart that serves
is beautiful,
that steady heart unchanged.

기쁠 때나 슬플 때나
속상할 때조차도

쉬지 않고 기도하는
그 모습이 참 곱다

우리 아내는 참 곱다

지금의 행복에 감사하고
늘 채워 주심에 감사하고

용서하고 사랑하는
부드러운 솜이불 같은 마음

하나님 바라보고
하나님 사랑하는

그 마음이 참 곱다

In joy and in sorrow,
even when hurt,
even then—

the way she prays without ceasing
is truly beautiful.

My wife is truly beautiful.

Grateful for the happiness of today,
grateful for being filled,
again and again.

A heart that forgives and loves,
soft like a warm quilt.

A heart that looks to God,
that loves God—

that heart
is truly beautiful.

Written in a sleepless dawn in San Francisco, inside a quiet hotel room.

약_藥으로 사는 인생

고지혈증 처방에 약을 먹기 시작한 지
어언 두 해

이번엔 혈압이 높다 하여 또 다른 약 처방 받아
한 움큼 손에 들고 보니

이젠 약으로 사는 인생

끼니 안 거르고 밥 챙겨 먹고
맛난 김치전에 막걸리 한 잔이면
족한 인생인 줄 알았더니

이젠 약 없인 안되는 인생

Life on Medicine

It's been two years now
since I started pills for high cholesterol.

This time,
they say my blood pressure is high—
another prescription, a new bottle.
Holding a handful of pills
in my palm, I realize—

this is a life lived on medicine.

I thought life was simple:
never skip a meal,
a good bowl of rice,
a crispy kimchi pancake,
one glass of *makgeolli*—
enough.

But now,
it's a life that doesn't work
without pills.

종심從心 바라보는 나이 이제야 알아가는 인생
조심스레 조금씩 다가가는 인생

새로이 친구된 약藥과 더불어

Only now,

at an age that looks back

around seventy years old,

do I begin to understand

this life—

a life approached carefully,

step by step.

Together

with medicine—

my newly made friend.

Written while holding a handful of prescription bags, letting the thoughts settle.

언어

도무지 알아들을 수가 없다
지들은 재밌게 얘기 하는데

언어는 나라마다
왜 이렇게 다를까

바벨탑의 원죄 때문인가
하나님의 진노 때문인가

끼리끼리는 통하고
따로따로는 막히고

이방인 전도의 명을 받은 바울은
참으로 이 문제를 어떻게 했을까

해외에서 마주한 여러 나라 여행객을 바라보며 문뜩 느낀 단상斷想 _ 2511

Language

I can't understand a single word.

They're laughing,

having a great time—

but none of it reaches me.

Why is language so different

from country to country?

Is it the original sin of the Tower of Babel?

The wrath of God?

Those who belong together understand each other.

Those set apart are shut out.

Paul,

given the calling to preach to the nations—

how did he ever cross this divide?

Written while watching travelers from many nations abroad—
a sudden thought caught and set down.

엎치락뒤치락

현실과 동떨어진 기괴한 생각들
뒤엉킨 실타래처럼 얽히고설켜

밤마다 엎치락뒤치락
뒤숭숭한 꿈으로

피하고 싶은 현실 같은 꿈
마주하고 싶지 않은 꿈같은 현실

야곱은 밤새워 천사와 씨름하고
나는 꿈 속에서 사탄과 낑낑대고

비몽사몽 뒤척이다 먼동이 트네
꿈인가 생시인가 자꾸 눈을 비빈다

밤잠을 설친 날 비몽사몽간에 기록하다 _ 2410

Toss and Turn

Strange thoughts,
detached from reality,
tangled and knotted like twisted threads.

Night after night,
I toss and turn,
pulled into restless dreams.

Dreams that feel like reality—
reality that feels like a dream
I don't want to face.

Jacob wrestled an angel through the night.
I wrestle Satan inside my sleep.

Half-awake, half-lost,
I turn and turn until dawn breaks.
Is this a dream, or waking life?
I rub my eyes again and again.

Written in a haze, after a sleepless night— somewhere between dream and waking.

여름날

햇살 쨍쨍 내리쬐는
뜨거운 여름날

등줄기 가슴팍 타고 흐르는
땀방울 또 땀방울

덥다 더워
아 더워 죽겠다

아니다 아니야
생각을 고쳐먹자

흐르는 땀방울도 감사하고
강렬한 태양도 감사하구나

여름의 무더위와 감사를 얽어보다 _ 2407

Summer Time

Blazing sunlight
pouring down—
on a scorching summer day.

Down my back, across my chest,
beads of sweat—
then more sweat.

So hot.
Too hot.
Damn, I'm burning up.

No, no—
wait.
Change your mind.

Even these drops of sweat,
I'm grateful.
Even this blazing sun,
I'm grateful.

Written while weaving together the heat of summer and a moment of gratitude.

여름날 : 댓글

햇살 쨍쨍 내리쬐는
뜨거운 여름날

*: 뜨거운 여름날을 아시오니
  아직 젊으십니다.*

등줄기 가슴팍 타고 흐르는
땀방울 또 땀방울

*: 땀방울이 타고 흐를 정도이니
  아직 청춘이십니다.*

덥다 더워
아 더워 죽겠다

*: 더워 죽겠다고 성을 내시오니
  아직 청년이십니다.*

Summer Time

: The Elder Han's Comment

Blazing sunlight

pouring down—

on a scorching summer day.

: If you can still call it scorching,

you are still young.

Down my back, across my chest,

beads of sweat—

then more sweat.

: If sweat can still run its course,

you are still in your prime.

So hot, so hot—

Damn, I'm burning up.

: If you can grumble about the heat,

you are still a young man.

아니다 아니야
생각을 고쳐먹자

: 생각의 전환을 하시오니
　아직 소년이십니다.

흐르는 땀방울도 감사하고
강렬한 태양도 감사하구나

: 감사의 열정이 있으시니
　역시 믿음의 산 증인이십니다.

No, no—

wait.

Change your mind.

: If you can shift your thinking,
you are still a boy at heart.

Even these drops of sweat,

I'm grateful.

Even this blazing sun,

I'm grateful.

: If gratitude still burns within you,
then truly—
you are a living witness of faith.

Commented by the Elder K.S Han

여행

돌아갈 때가 되니
여행이 아쉽구나

흙으로 돌아갈 때
인생 또한 아쉽겠지

여행 마지막 날, 호텔방에서 집으로 돌아갈 가방을 꾸리며 _ 2409

Journey

When it's time
to go back,
the journey already
feel like a loss.

When it's time
to return to dust,
life itself
will feel the same.

Written on the final night of a trip,
packing a suitcase in a hotel room, preparing to go home.

여행에 대하여

여행이란 무엇일까

설렘?
힐링Healing?
식도락食道樂?

아님 결국

너 거기 가봤니?
난 거기 가봤어!

은근한 깨알자랑
더도 덜도 말고

젊은 날의 추억이 서린 미국 필라델피아에 있는 Drexel University를 아내와
함께 둘러보다가 _ 2310

About Travel

What is travel, really?

Anticipation?
Healing?
Good food?

Or in the end—

Have you been there?
I've been there.

A quiet, tiny boast,
nothing more,
nothing less.

Written while walking with my wife around Drexel University in Philadelphia,
a place filled with memories from younger days.

예배당 2

살기 위해
나는 여기에 왔다

하지만
죽어 가는 것 같다

그래도 또 발걸음 옮긴다
예배당으로

살기 위해

아니
날마다 죽기 위해

A Chapel II

To live,
I came here.

And yet—
it feels like
I am dying.

Still,
I take another step,
toward the chapel.

To live.

No—
to die,
day after day.

Written after reading 「the Notebooks of Malte Laurids Brigge」,
leaving behind a single line.

요게벳의 노래

생때같은 자식 갈대바구니에 담아
강물에 띄워 보내는 엄마의 마음

둥둥 떠내려가는 그 모습 바라보며
요게벳은 과연 어떤 생각을 했을까?

명령에 순종하여
손에 칼을 든 아브라함

겹치는 듯 두 모습 가슴을 치네
깨달음 있으라 그 크신 예비하심

모세의 어머니 요게벳의 이야기를 구약에서 읽으며 _ 2401

Songs by Jochebed

A mother places her living child

into a basket of reeds,

and sets him adrift on the river.

Watching him float away,

what thoughts must have filled

Jochebed's heart?

Obedience to a command—

Abraham, knife in hand.

The two images overlap,

striking the chest.

May there be understanding—

of that great provision,

so carefully prepared.

Written while reading the story of Jochebed, the mother of Moses, in the Old Testament.

유붕자원방래 불역낙호 有朋自遠方來, 不亦樂乎

멀리 서울에서
후배가 찾아왔다

졸작拙作 두 권을 읽고 너무 얘기가 하고 싶었단다
그저 무슨 이야기든 듣고 싶단다

죽음 이야기
천국 소망 이야기

다 뱉아 놓을 수 없는
가슴 속 깊은 이야기

그저 그런 우리네 인생에
선물 같은 이야기

Isn't It a Joy to See a Friend from Afar?

From far away—

from Seoul—

a younger friend comes to visit.

He says he read my humble books, two of them,

and couldn't stop wanting to talk.

He says

he just wanted to listen—

to anything.

Stories of death.

Stories of hope for heaven.

Stories too deep to spill all at once,

kept in the chest.

In our ordinary lives,

stories that feel like gifts.

이런저런 이야기
시골 막걸리 한 사발에 담아

오늘도 감사하며 기쁨으로 나눈다
마음으로 찾아온 사랑의 후배와 함께

This and that,

poured into a single bowl of country *makgeolli*.

Today again,

with gratitude and joy, I share them—

with a younger friend

who came not just in body, but in heart.

Written while sharing a bowl of *makgeolli* with a younger friend who came all the way from Seoul.

유월의 끝자락에서

벌써 반 년이?

해가 거듭할수록
속도감이 장난 아니다

뭐든 다 이룰 듯한
새해 첫날 마음 여전한데

잡은 듯 새나간 듯
세월 훌쩍 뛰어넘어

이미 반 년이?

At the End of June

Already—

half a year?

With every passing year,

the speed is unreal.

That New Year's Day resolve—

feeling like anything was possible—

it's still here.

And yet—

as if I had it,

as if it slipped away—

time vaults ahead,

and already—

half a year?

기대하며 반 년
기다리며 반 년

유월의 끝자락에서
그녀의 이름 소환한다

나의 반녀니

올해도 어김없이 찾아온 유월의 마지막 날, 새해 첫날의 감정을 떠올리며 적
다 _ 2506

Half a year of hoping.
Half a year of waiting.

At the very end of June,
I call her name—

My half-year love.

이사

아파트 같은 층 수년을 같이 지내던
노년의 부부가 이사를 갔다

그리고 어린 아이 둘과 함께
젊은 부부가 이사를 온단다

물갈이인가?
인생은 돌고 돌아 또 그 자리

이삿짐 나가는 노부부의 모습에
리모델링한다며 분주한 젊은 부부 모습에

언젠간 같은 모습일
우리 집 우리 부부와 겹친다

A Move

On the same floor of our apartment,
a couple, now elderly, who lived beside us for years,
has moved away.

And now—
a young couple moves in, with two small children.

Is this a replacing?
Life turns, and returns to the same place.

Watching the elderly couple's belongings
being carried out,
watching the young couple—
busy, talking about remodeling—

I see us.
Our home. Our future.
As we'll one day be.

들고 나고
나고 들고

이 세상에 보내져서 감사히 지냈으니
머잖아 나도 저 천국으로 이사가리라

Carried out. Carried in.
Out and in. In and out.

Sent into this world,
we lived with gratitude.

Before long,
I too will move—
to heaven.

Written while watching neighbors come and go through moving day on the same floor.

일등석

항공사 업그레이드로 감사한 마음으로
쭈우욱 기지개를 켠다 의자를 일자로 펼치고

참 좋다 일등석
하늘을 나는 제법 큰 깡통 속에서

갖은 호사를 누린다
진수성찬은 덤으로

즐거움은 돈으로 사는 것인가
은혜로 주어지는 것인가

같은 공간임에도 한 쪽은 뻗대고
다른 쪽은 쪼그리고

First Class

Upgraded by the airline—
grateful,
I stretch all the way out,
lay the seat flat.

It's great.
First class.
Inside this pretty big flying metal can,
high above the clouds,

I enjoy
every possible comfort.
A feast,
thrown in for free.

Is pleasure something you buy with money,
or something you receive as grace?

Same cabin—
one side stretched out,
the other curled in.

돈을 탐할 것인가
영을 따를 것인가

교만을 위선으로 포장한 채
쭈우욱 사지 늘리니 그저 시원할 따름이구나

깨달음 있으라
그대 스노브Snob여

Do you chase wealth,

or do you follow the Spirit?

I wrap arrogance in the name of privilege,

stretch my limbs again—

ah,

it feels good.

Let there be insight.

You snob.

Written while lying flat on a flight to the Holy Land tour. (KE957, seats 01A and 01B).

외로운 소나무

태평양 해안 바위 위
소나무 하나 외로이

긴 세월 해풍 넘어
온갖 이야기 깃든

홀로 외로이 버텨온 무게감
험한 비바람 견뎌온 의연함

보듬어주고 토닥여주고픈
해안 바위 위 외로움 하나

10여 년 만에 다시 찾은 몬트레이 17마일 드라이브길에 마주한, 전엔 왕성하
던 소나무 이파리 일부가 이젠 완연히 변색된 모습을 바라보며 짠한 마음에
적다 _ 2508

The Lone Cypress

On a rocky cliff along the Pacific coast,
a single cypress stands alone.

Crossing decades of salty wind,
holding countless stories.

The weight of standing alone for so long.
The dignity of enduring fierce storms and rain.

I want to gather it close,
to pat it gently—
that loneliness,
standing on the coastal rock.

Written while revisiting the 17-Mile Drive in Monterey after more than ten years— seeing how the once-lush needles had quietly faded, and feeling a sudden ache.

Chapter 1

작은 글 모음

Ⅲ 자 - 하

배

자

ㅡ

하

작은 가방

왼팔 왼다리 바람맞은 남편은
암 덩어리 몸에 숨긴 아내 배웅 받으며

작은 가방 꾸러미 하나 의지하여
짐짓 태연한 체 요양원으로 떠났다

인생이 꾸러미 하나인가?
그 많던 영욕榮辱 다 어디로 가고

버려라 내려 놓으라
어디선가 들리는 하늘의 웅성거림

태초로 돌아가자
시작을 맞이하자

죽음 한가득 구겨 담긴
작은 가방 하나 들고

문득문득 떠오르는 아버지 손에 들린 가방— 요양병원으로 떠나가시던 아버지의 뒷모습 _ 2210

A Small Bag

A husband,
his left arm and left leg failing,
is seen off by his wife—
a body hiding a mass of cancer.

With only a small bag to lean on,
he leaves for the nursing home,
forcing calm onto his face.

Is life just one small bundle?
All that glory and disgrace—
where did it all go?

Let it go.
Lay it down.
Somewhere, a murmur from heaven.

Return to the beginning.
Meet the start again.

Holding a small bag,
stuffed and crumpled with death.

Written from the image that returns again and again—
my father's back, walking away toward a nursing hospital, a bag in his hand.

잠 1

해지고 어둠이 내려 앉으면
잠이라는 손님이 나를 이끈다

죽음의 방문인가
삶의 시소인가

하루의 시작 알람음과 함께
눈 비비며 깨어나 쫓아내지만

몰아내고 걷어차도 다시 찾아온다
땅거미지면 어김없이 하품과 함께

언제까지일까 이 달콤한 반복은
사위 깜깜해지면 또 찾아오겠지

Sleeping I

When the sun sets and darkness settles in,
a guest called sleep takes me by the hand.

Is it a visit from death,
or a seesaw of life?

With the alarm—
the signal of a new day—
I rub my eyes, wake up, and chase it away.

But no matter how I push it off,
kick it aside, it comes back again—
faithfully, with a yawn as dusk falls.

How long will this sweet repetition last?
When everything turns pitch-dark,
it will come again, won't it?

Written after waking from sleep,
rubbing my eyes, and setting down a single line.

잠 2

간밤에
푸욱 잘 잤다

천국도
과연 이렇게

Sleeping II

Last night—
I slept
so deeply.

Heaven, too,
could it be
like this?

Written after waking from a long, restful sleep—
a quiet hope surfacing on its own.

잡초

참 대단하다

단단한 포장도로 좁게 갈라진 틈새에도
파릇파릇 연둣빛 새순을 틔운다

억세게 질긴 생명력
밟아도 밟혀도 비집고 올라오는

척박한 환경이면 어떠리
한 줌 흙이면 족한 걸

내 인생도 잡초만 같았음 좋겠다
하늘나라 가는 그 날까지

홀로 고속도로를 운전하다가 도로 위에 언뜻언뜻 보이는 잡초를 바라보며 _
2307

Weeds

Remarkable—

truly remarkable.

Even in the narrow cracks of hardened pavement,

fresh green shoots push their way through.

A fierce, stubborn will to live—

stepped on, pressed down, yet rising again.

So what if the ground is barren?

A single handful of soil is enough.

I hope my life can be like weeds—

until the day I walk toward heaven.

Written while driving alone on the highway, catching sight—
again and again—
of weeds breaking through the road.

짜증

시도 때도 없이 아부지는
왜 그리 짜증을 내셨을까

돌아가신 지 벌써 몇 해건만
지워도 다시 떠오르는 편린들

얼마나 힘드셨을까 오마니는
평생 그 짜증 다 받아주면서

어느 날 문득 돌아보니
판박이 하나 딱 나왔다

짜증을 내고 있는 나를 보며
나는 또다시 확 짜증이 난다

무시로 표출되는 짜증내는 나를 돌아보다가 깜짝 놀라 적다 (시 37:8) _
2507

Irritation

Why was my father so irritable—
all the time?

It's been years since he passed,
yet the fragments return,
no matter how hard I try to erase them.

How hard it must have been for my mother,
taking in that irritation for a lifetime.

And then one day, I turn around—
and there it is.
A perfect copy.
Me.

I catch myself getting irritated.
And seeing myself like that,
I get—
irritated all over again.

Written in sudden shock, catching myself in a moment of irritation— a quiet reflection inspired by Psalm 37:8.

좋은 친구

치열한 인생 투쟁 그 여정에서
신만큼 좋은 친구 어디 있을까

언제 어디서나 불러 외쳐도
언제나 어김없이 응답해 주는

늘 내 곁에 있는 참 좋은 친구
손잡고 동행하는 나의 길동무

좋은 친구란 누구일까 생각해 보니 이만한 친구가 없구나! (요 15:15) _
2508

Good Friend

In the fierce struggle
of this life's journey,
who could be a better friend
than God Himself?

Call out—
anytime, anywhere—
and the answer comes,
without fail.

A truly good friend,
always by my side—
my companion on the road,
hand in hand.

Written while wondering who a good friend really is— and realizing there is none greater. (John 15:15)

첫눈

첫눈이 내린다
바람에 실려 이리저리 날린다

한여름 무더위가 실리고
가을의 실한 알곡도 실리고

첫눈이 내린다
하얗게 온 세상을 덮을 기세로

죄 많은 인간들 용서함인가
하늘나라 신들의 값없는 베풂인가

첫눈이 내린다
참고 참은 억눌림 한꺼번에 폭발하듯

기세 좋게 쏟아붓는다
공중에서 공중으로

First Snow

The first snow falls.
Carried by the wind,
it drifts—
this way, that way.

It carries the heat of midsummer.
It carries the full grain of autumn.

The first snow falls,
as if to cover the whole world in white.

Is it forgiveness for sinful humanity?
Or the gods of heaven,
giving freely, without price?

The first snow falls—
like a dam breaking,
all the restraint held back too long released at once.

It pours down with force,
from sky to sky.

Written while watching the first snow fall heavily outside the window on November 27, 2024.

첫사랑

샤론의 장미 투영된 듯
순수하고 아련한 마음

긴 세월 흘러도
지워지지 않는

첫사랑 그 강렬함
삶의 에너지 되어

목 축이고 또 걸어가네
그 음성 그 입술 그 첫 기억으로

예배하며 찬송하다가 처음 만난 그 순간이 떠올라 기록하다 _ 2509

First Love

As if the Rose of Sharon
were reflected there—
a heart
pure
and softly trembling.

Though long years have passed,
it does not fade.

The fierce intensity
of first love
becomes the energy of life.

I quench my thirst
and keep walking—
by that voice,
those lips,
that very first memory.

Written during worship, while singing a hymn,
as the moment of first meeting suddenly returned.

추석 명절

추석 명절 동네 앞산
부모산성 오르니

사찰 터줏대감
냥이 홀로 반긴다

후두둑 떨어지는 알밤
청량한 자연의 소리

그 소리에 놀라 달아났는지
가방 멘 사람들 다 주워 간 탓인지

언제부턴가 부모산엔
다람쥐 한 마리 보이지 않는다

Chuseok

On Chuseok morning, I climb the small mountain
in front of my neighborhood—
Bumo Fortress.

A temple's old guardian,
a lone cat, greets me.

Chestnuts fall—
thud, thud—
the crisp sound of nature.

Did the noise scare them away,
or did the backpacked hikers
take them all?

At some point,
not a single squirrel
is to be seen on this mountain.

지속되는 무더위 속
땀 범벅 흠뻑 젖은 몸

어릴 적 다람쥐 추억에
먼저 가신 님들 그리움에

땀방울 눈물방울
뒤범벅된 채로

한 해 명절이 그렇게 또
아련히 내 앞을 지나가고 있다

In the lingering heat,
my body drenched,
soaked in sweat.

With childhood memories of squirrels,
with longing for those who went ahead of me—

sweat drops,
tear drops,
mixed together.

Another holiday passes by like that,
softly,
achingly,
right in front of me.

치통

이가 아프다
잇몸도 욱신욱신하다

위턱 최 안쪽 어금니 부근
가만히 있어도 쿡쿡 찌른다

진통제 항생제 버텨보건만
처방을 비웃듯 졸라 아프다

살살 달래 가며 써보라는 젊은 치의사
그게 맘대로 되냐 속으로 언짢은 노인

Toothache

My tooth hurts.
My gums throb—
pulse after pulse.

Way back, the very last molar on the upper jaw—
even doing nothing, it stabs,
again and again.

Painkillers. Antibiotics.
I try to endure.
They mock the prescription,
the pain just tightens its grip.

The young dentist says,
Use it gently, try to live with it.
Easy for you to say—
I grumble inside, an old man annoyed.

아픈 이는 뽑아내야 옳지 않나
그래도 붙어있는 이에 감사해야 하나

이노무 치통을
우찌 통치해야 할꼬

If it hurts,

shouldn't it be pulled out?

Or should I still be grateful

for what remains attached?

This cursed toothache—

how on earth

am I supposed to rule it?

Written while suffering through an unbearable toothache.

코비드 19 그 이후

참 상쾌하다
마스크 하나 벗었을 뿐인데

참 유쾌하다
보고픈 친구 즐거운 식사가

손톱 옆 거스러미 떼어낸 듯
푹푹 찌는 무더위 속 냉욕을 한 듯

자유함은 인간의 궁극인가
원하고 바라는 것이 자유함인가

코로나 세계를 겪으며
삶의 소중함을 배웠다

코로나 어려움에도 감사가 있거늘
일상의 어려움이 어찌 어려움이랴

마스크 쓰고 산책하다가 문득 떠오른 코로나 시절 생각에 _ 2505

COVID-19 and Beyond

It feels so refreshing—
just taking off a mask.

It feels so good—
a meal with a friend I've missed.

Like tearing off a hangnail
beside the fingernail,
like plunging into a cold bath in suffocating heat.

Is freedom the ultimate human desire?
Is it what we seek and long for most?

Living through the world of COVID,
I learned the value of life.

If gratitude existed even in the hardships of COVID,
how could the struggles of ordinary days
still be called hardships?

Written while walking with a mask on, as memories of the COVID years
suddenly surfaced.

코이의 법칙

물고기조차도 그릇의 크기를 안다는데
나는 왜 아직도 그걸 모를까

뱀 핑계 대고
여자 핑계 대고

삶의 본질을 놓치고
복잡하게만 생각하기 때문일까

그저 믿고 따르자
단순함을 회복하자

코이에게서도
배움이 있지 않은가

우연히 방송에서 코이의 법칙을 듣다가 적다 _ 2307

Koi's Law

They say even a fish
knows the size of its bowl.

So why—
why don't I?

I blame the snake.
I blame the woman.

Maybe it's because I miss the essence of life,
thinking everything too complicated.

So—
let's just believe.
Let's just follow.
Let's recover simplicity.

If even a koi has something to teach us,
don't we?

Written after hearing, by chance, about *Koi's Law* on a broadcast.

파스칼의 내기

신은 있는가
없는가

하늘에 있는가 땅에 있는가
아님 우리 마음에 있는가

없는가
그럼 왜 믿는가

만족을 얻고자 함인가
위로를 받고자 함인가

파스칼은
왜 내기를 했을까

파스칼의 내기를 읽다가 적어보다 _ 2405

Pascal's Wager

Does God exist—
or not?

In the sky?
On the earth?
Or somewhere inside our hearts?

If He does not—
then why believe?

For satisfaction?
For comfort?

Why, then,
did *Blaise Pascal* place a wager?

Written after reading *Pascal's Wager*, letting the questions sit where they may.

평안 平安

이만하면 잘 살았다 위안이 될 법한데
무엇이 그리 아쉬워 아직도 붙잡을까

산등성이 풀의 꽃이 피고 또 지듯
한 번 왔다 한 번 가는 인생 여정에

좋아하는 사람도 사랑하는 사람도
때론 싫어하는 사람조차도

Peace

By now,
this should be enough
to say, I lived well.
So why—
what is it that I still cling to?

Like flowers on the hillside grass that bloom, then fade,
this life's journey—
we come once, we go once.

People I liked.
People I loved.
Even those I sometimes resented—

만나고 부대끼다 이만큼이나 왔으니
공수레공수거空手來空手去 이만하면 지족知足이라

내 눈 속 여전한 들보 뽑아내며
남은 여정 뚜벅뚜벅 감사함으로 따르리

meeting them,

colliding with them,

I've come this far.

Empty-handed I came.

Empty-handed I will go.

This should be enough—

contentment at last.

Pulling out the beam still lodged in my own eyes,

I will walk the rest of the road

step by step,

following with gratitude.

Written after a meeting that revealed how hard it is to let go of past glory (Matthew 7:3).

하얀 눈

하얀 눈이 밤새 소복이 내렸다
그 위를 걷는다 발자국 남기며

뽀드득 뽀드득
그리고 또 뽀드득 뽀드득

새하얀 눈만큼
소리 또한 참 하야다

아무 흠 없는 하아얀 눈 위에
남겨지는 걸음걸음 그 자국들

깨어 있자 눈을 크게 뜨자
긴 호흡으로 하늘을 바라보자

White Snow

White snow fell softly through the night,
piling up.
I walk across it,
leaving footprints behind.

Crunch.
Crunch.
And again—
crunch, crunch.

As white as the snow itself,
the sound is white too.

On this flawless field of white,
each step leaves its mark.

Stay awake.
Open your eyes wide.
Take a long breath and look up to the sky.

Written while walking along a snowy path at dawn.

행복

오늘 저녁엔 무얼 먹지요?
아내와 나의 찐 대화

생 두부 한 모 사오실래요?
전라도 처형표 맛난 김치는 언제나 집에

막걸리 한 병 마트에서 구해오니
풍요로운 포만감 우리는 이미 부자로세

탱글탱글 두부 한 모 상큼한 김치 반 포기
그리고 생 막걸리 한 잔

엉뚱한 곳 뒤진다고 찾아지나요
행복의 끝판왕 바로 이것이로세

자녀들 다 떠나고 둘만 남은 집안에서 늘 일어나는 노인들의 다반사 중 하나
를 기록하다 _ 2412

Happiness

What should we eat tonight?
A real, honest conversation between my wife and me.

How about a block of fresh tofu?
There's always good kimchi at home,
from my sister-in-law in Jeolla.

I pick up a bottle of *makgeolli*
from the market—
and just like that, we're already rich.

A firm block of tofu,
half a head of crisp kimchi,
and one glass of fresh *makgeolli*.

Do you really think you'll find happiness
digging around in strange places?
The final boss of happiness—
it's right here.

Written as one of those everyday moments in a house left with just the two of us, like old people, after the children have all gone.

힐링

힐링
그것은 멈춤의 실천

힐링
그것은 영육의 이완

힐링
그것은 채움의 만족

힐링
그것은 변명의 거부

힐링
그것은 또 다른 시작점

Healing

Healing—
the practice of stopping.

Healing—
the loosening of body and soul.

Healing—
the satisfaction of being filled.

Healing—
the refusal of excuses.

Healing—
another starting point.

Written while walking aimlessly along the San Francisco shoreline, finding quiet comfort for the heart.

CES 2023

세상을 리딩Leading한다는 CES 2023
그 현장에 빠져들어

감사하다 여기까지 이끌어 주심에
참 감사하다 인간에게 능력 주심에

끝 모를 색다름에 흠뻑 젖어
또 감사하다 나의 교만을 일깨워 주니

어디까지일까 한계를 넘어
빠져들어 흠뻑 젖어 가상과 현실을 넘나들며

다시 힘을 내자 기운을 내자
하나님 주신 능력으로

2023년 1월 미국 Las Vegas에서 개최된 CES 참관기 _ 2301

CES 2023

CES 2023—
they say it leads the world.
And there I was,
drawn in, caught inside the current.

Grateful—
for being led this far.
So Grateful—
for the abilities given to humankind.

Soaked in endless newness,
I find myself grateful again— .
for being shaken awake from my own pride.

How far does it go?
Beyond limits, slipping in,
fully immersed,
crossing back and forth between virtual and real.

So—
let's gather strength again.
Let's rise once more.
With the abilities God has given.

Written after attending the Consumer Electronics Show in Las Vegas, January 2023.

7월 4일

일하러 떠나온 날
그 날이 July 4th

Happy Birthday America
미국 전체가 말 그대로 축제

국회의사당 앞에서
할렐루야 부르고

IT메카 산호세의 밤하늘
화려하게 수놓은 드론쇼

뉴욕 맨하탄 허드슨강 위로는
화려한 불꽃놀이 그야말로 장관

July 4th

I left for work—
and that day was July 4th.

Happy Birthday, America.
The whole country,
a living festival.

In front of the Capitol,
voices rise—
hallelujah.

Over the night sky of San Jose,
the IT capital,
drones stitch light into darkness.

Above the Hudson River over Manhattan,
fireworks bloom—
a breathtaking spectacle.

어른 아이 백인 흑인
손에 손에 성조기 들고

다 같이 함께 웃고 즐기는
행복한 얼굴 활기찬 모습

즐길 줄 아는 국민
일할 줄 아는 국민

주여 이 나라를 축복하소서
주여 어머니에게 영원한 안식을 주소서

Adults and children,
Black and white,
flags in every hand.

Laughing together.
Celebrating together.
Faces alive with joy.

A people who know how to enjoy.
A people who know how to work.

Lord, bless this land.
Lord, grant my mother eternal rest.

Written while on a business trip in the U.S. encountering July 4th—
America's Independence Day, and the day my mother went home to
heaven, more than ten years ago.

Chapter 2

야고보서 묵상
Book of James' Meditation

1 - 5 장

야고보서 묵상

행함으로 증명되는 믿음
Faith Proven by Works

1 - 5 장

읽기 전에 일러두기

　본 내용은 2023년 8월 23일부터 2024년 1월 31일까지 약 5개월 동안 새벽마다 야고보서를 하루에 한 절 읽으면서 느낀 바를 소그룹 형제자매들과 '한 줄 묵상'이라는 제목으로 함께 나눈 은혜를 개제한 것입니다. 여러분도 야고보서를 통해 행함의 위대함을 깨우치며 하나님의 크신 복을 누리길 소망합니다.

　문득 산티아고 순례길(El Camino de Santiago)을 걸어 보고 싶은 마음이 드네요. 실천하고 안 하고는 나의 행함에 달려 있겠지요?

"우리는 그가 만드신 바라 그리스도 예수안에서 선한 일을 위하여 지으심을 받은 자니 이 일은 하나님이 전에 예비하사 우리로 그 가운데서 행하게 하려 하심이니라" (엡 2:10)

야고보서 1장

야고보서 1:1
하나님과 주 예수 그리스도의 종 야고보는 흩어져
있는 열두 지파에게 문안하노라

: 스스로 종이라 칭하는 야고보 선지자의 당당함을 배웁
니다. 더하여 그 인사성을 배웁니다. 인사만 잘해도 먹고
산다는 말이 있습니다. 미움이 있습니까? 용서하고 서로
문안하며 아침을 열면 좋겠습니다.

야고보서 1:2
내 형제들아 너희가 여러 가지 시험을 당하거든 온
전히 기쁘게 여기라

: 환난은 인내를, 인내는 연단을, 연단은 소망을 이룸(롬
5:3-4)을 믿고 기쁨으로 여기게 하십시오. 예수님의 이
름으로 기도합니다. 아멘

야고보서 1:3
이는 너희 믿음의 시련이 인내를 만들어 내는 줄 너
희가 앎이라

: 실제로 맞고 자라면 맷집이 세집니다. 운동도 한계를
넘어서야 내 근육이 됩니다. 믿음이라는 정신세계도 마찬

가지입니다. 시련이 와도 환난이 닥쳐도 믿음과 행함으로 이겨내도록 나를 인도 하소서.

야고보서 1:4
인내를 온전히 이루라 이는 너희로 온전하고 구비하여 조금도 부족함이 없게 하려 함이라

: 20억년 전에 생성되었다는 미국 그랜드캐니언(Grand Canyon)의 장엄함을 바라보노라면 그 웅장함과 켜켜이 쌓인 지층의 무게감에 경이로움을 느낍니다. 한 치의 오차도 없이 조금도 부족함이 없게 한 하나님의 손길을 느낍니다. 하물며 사람에게 모자람이 있겠습니까?

야고보서 1:5
너희 중에 누구든지 지혜가 부족하거든 모든 사람에게 후히 주시고 꾸짖지 아니하시는 하나님께 구하라 그리하면 주시리라

: "구하는 이마다 얻을 것이요"(마 7:8) 라고 하신 하나님의 말씀을 믿습니다. 세상을 의지하지 않고 오직 하나님께 기도로 간구하게 하옵소서.

야고보서 1:6
오직 믿음으로 구하고 조금도 의심하지 말라 의심하는 자는 마치 바람에 밀려 요동하는 바다 물결 같으니

: 염려가 병이라면 믿음은 약입니다. 믿음으로 평안을 누리길 원합니다. 주님 도와주세요.

야고보서 1:7
이런 사람은 무엇이든지 주께 얻기를 생각하지 말라

: 기도하고도 종종 그 결과를 의심하는 때가 있습니다. 하나님의 때를 참지 못하고 조급증이 들 때가 있습니다. 서두르면 이스마엘을 낳고 기다리면 이삭을 낳습니다. 주님, 오직 믿음으로 구하고 기다릴 줄 아는 지혜를 주십시오.

야고보서 1:8
두 마음을 품어 모든 일에 정함이 없는 자로다

: 두 마음을 품은 적이 종종 있었음을 반성합니다. 될까? 의심한 적이 많았음을 회개합니다. 주여 용서해 주시고 정함이 있는 삶으로 인도하소서.

야고보서 1:9
낮은 형제는 자기의 높음을 자랑하고

: 내가 낮다고 의기소침意氣鎖沈하여 풀이 죽어있지 말고 그 위치에서 하나님이 나에게 주신 은사대로 감사하며 살라는 말씀 아닐까요? 주어진 처소處所에서 오직 복음으로 살기를 원합니다.

야고보서 1:10
부한 자는 자기의 낮아짐을 자랑할지니 이는 그가
풀의 꽃과 같이 지나감이라

: 영원한 것은 없습니다. 돈이 많고 세상 좋은 물건 다
가진 자라도 풀의 꽃이 지듯 언젠가는 사라집니다. 오직
하나님의 말씀만이 영원합니다.
 "진리를 알지니 진리가 너희를 자유롭게 하리라" (요
8:32)

야고보서 1:11
해가 돋고 뜨거운 바람이 불어 풀을 말리면 꽃이 떨
어져 그 모양의 아름다움이 없어지나니 부한 자도
그 행하는 일에 이와 같이 쇠잔하리라

: 우리 모두는 언젠가는 죽음에 이를 것이니 살아있는 동
안 하나님 바라기에 힘써야 합니다. 돈이 그리스도가 되
면 안 되고 자랑이 그리스도가 되면 안 되고 남의 시선이
나 명예가 그리스도가 되면 안 됩니다. 오직 말씀 따라
살게 하여 주십시오.

야고보서 1:12
시험을 참는 자는 복이 있나니 이는 시련을 견디어
낸 자가 주께서 자기를 사랑하는 자들에게 약속하신
생명의 면류관을 얻을 것이기 때문이라

: 살다 보면 여러 어려움이 닥치기 마련입니다. 그러나,

어떤 어려움이 있어도 우리가 견딜 만큼만 주시는 하나님을 믿고 의지하여 오늘도 세상에서 승리하는 삶이 되길 기도합니다.

야고보서 1:13
사람이 시험을 받을 때에 내가 하나님께 시험을 받는다 하지 말지니 하나님은 악에게 시험을 받지도 아니하시고 친히 아무도 시험하지 아니하시느니라

: 어떤 어려움에 처했을 때 우리는 종종 시험에 들었다고 말하며 힘들어합니다. 때론 하나님을 원망합니다. 하지만 이 또한 감사해야 합니다. 인내와 연단은 소망을 이루기 때문입니다. 시험을 이기고 승리하게 하소서.

야고보서 1:14
오직 각 사람이 시험을 받는 것은 자기 욕심에 끌려 미혹됨이니

: 만나에 욕심을 낸 결과기 이띠했습니끼? 벌레기 생기고 냄새가 나지 않았습니까? 야욕이나 과욕은 버리고 지족知足하고 자족自足할 줄 알아야 합니다. 욕심으로부터 자유롭기를 기도합니다.
"너희 각 사람은 먹을 만큼만 이것을 거둘지니"(출 16:16)

야고보서 1:15
욕심이 잉태한즉 죄를 낳고 죄가 장성한즉 사망을
낳느니라

: 각 사람에게 문제가 발생하고 어려움에 봉착하는 것은
스스로 자기 욕심에 끌려서 된 것입니다. 하나님 탓이 아
닙니다. 내 안에 살아 역사하시는 주님, 나를 욕심에 끌
리지 않도록 선한 영으로 인도하여 주십시오.

야고보서 1:16-17
내 사랑하는 형제들아 속지 말라 온갖 좋은 은사와
온전한 선물이 다 위로부터 빛들의 아버지께로부터
내려오나니 그는 변함도 없으시고 회전하는 그림자
도 없으시니라

: 탐욕과 분노와 어리석음은 우리가 늘 경계하며 살아야
할 것들입니다. 우리는 믿음과 감사와 사랑으로 살아야
합니다. 사랑하는 형제자매와 그 가정에 오늘도 주님의
은총과 평안이 함께 하기를 기도합니다.

야고보서 1:18
그가 그 피조물 중에 우리로 한 첫 열매가 되게 하
시려고 자기의 뜻을 따라 진리의 말씀으로 우리를
낳으셨느니라

: 하나님의 형상대로 지음 받은 우리는 늘 주님 안에 있
음을 깨닫고 그 말씀 따라 살아야 합니다. 곁길로 가다가
도 다시 돌아와야 합니다. 사도 바울의 회심(回心, Metanoia)

처럼 회개하고 회복되어야 합니다. 그 깊은 뜻을 따라 살
게 하소서.

야고보서 1:19
내 사랑하는 형제들아 너희가 알지니 사람마다 듣기
는 속히 하고 말하기는 더디 하며 성내기도 더디 하
라

: 상대방이 말할 때는 귀 기울여 잘 듣고 내가 말할 때는
한 번 더 생각하여 말하고 화는 백해무익임을 거듭 깨우
쳐 주십시오. 예수님 이름으로 기도합니다. 아멘

야고보서 1:20
사람이 성내는 것이 하나님의 의를 이루지 못함이라

: 화를 내면 하나님의 뜻은커녕 천국에 이르지 못한다고
합니다. 그래도 화를 내시겠습니까? 성질 따라 사는 인생
이 아니라 복음 따라 살기를 소망합니다.

야고보서 1:21
그러므로 모든 더러운 것과 넘치는 악을 내버리고
너희 영혼을 능히 구원할 바 마음에 심어진 말씀을
온유함으로 받으라

: 아멘

야고보서 1:22
너희는 말씀을 행하는 자가 되고 듣기만 하여 자신
을 속이는 자가 되지 말라

: 언행일치言行一致 즉, 말과 그에 따른 행동이 같아야 합
니다. 표리부동表裏不同하면 안됩니다. 자신을 속이는 것은
주님을 속이는 것입니다. 기회주의자가 되지 않게 우리를
믿음의 길로 인도하여 주십시오.

야고보서 1:23
누구든지 말씀을 듣고 행하지 아니하면 그는 거울로
자기의 생긴 얼굴을 보는 사람과 같아서

: 하루에 자기 얼굴을 거울로 몇 번이나 보시나요? 거울
속의 그 얼굴이 기억 나시나요? 호손(미국 작가)의 소설
『큰 바위 얼굴』이 생각납니다. 부단히 읽고 듣고 행하
려 노력했는지 아닌지 그 모습이 거울 속에 있습니다.
주님, 나의 가면을 벗겨 주세요.

야고보서 1: 24
제 자신을 보고 가서 그 모습이 어떠했는지를 곧 잊
어버리거니와

: '거울아 거울아 이 세상에서 누가 제일 예쁘니?' – 동
화 『백설공주』에 나오는 나르시시즘Narcissism에 빠진 왕
비의 독백입니다. 지나치게 자기 자신이 뛰어나다고 믿는
잘난 체하는 모습입니다.

주님, 교만을 버리고 겸손한 삶을 살도록 나를 지켜 주세
요.

야고보서 1:25
자유롭게 하는 온전한 율법을 들여다보고 있는 자는
듣고 잊어버리는 자가 아니요 실천하는 자니 이 사
람은 그 행하는 일에 복을 받으리라

: 'Freedom is not free' (자유는 거저 주어지는 것이 아니다)
– 미국 워싱턴 D..C..의 6.25 한국전쟁기념관에 적혀 있
는 문구입니다. 하나님 나라도 그냥 들어갈 수 있는 건
아니잖아요? 행함으로 복을 받는 믿음의 사람이 되길 기
도합니다.

야고보서 1:26
누구든지 스스로 경건하다 생각하며 자기 혀를 재갈
물리지 아니하고 자기 마음을 속이면 이 사람의 경
건은 헛것이라

: '세 치 혀를 조심하라' – 말조심하라는 얘기입니다. 세
상의 더러운 것은 다 입에서 나온다고 주님께서 말씀하셨
습니다. 자랑도, 속이는 말도 모두 배설물입니다. 배설물
은 오직 뒤로 나오는 은혜를 받으시길... 샬롬

야고보서 1:27
하나님 아버지 앞에서 정결하고 더러움이 없는 경건

은 곧 고아와 과부를 그 환난중에 돌보고 또 자기를
지켜 세속에 물들지 아니하는 그것이니라

: 어려운 이웃을 외면하지 말고 세상의 죄에 빠지지 말라
는 말씀입니다. 따뜻한 마음으로 내가 먼저 손 내밀게 하
십시오.

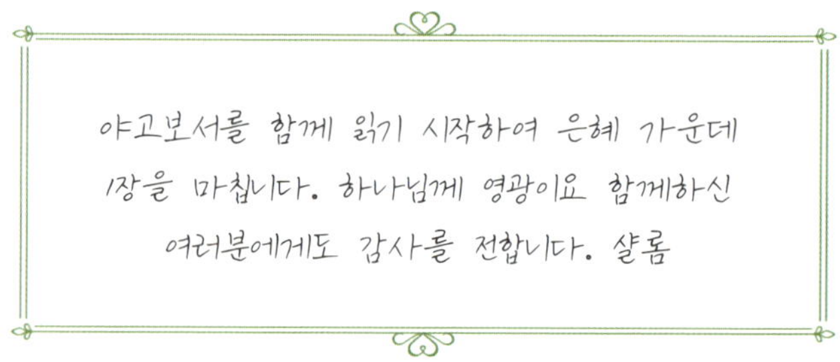

야고보서 2장

야고보서 2:1
내 형제들아 영광의 주 곧 우리 주 예수 그리스도에
대한 믿음을 너희가 가졌으니 사람을 차별하여 대하
지 말라

: 예수님은 이 땅에 계신 동안 세리도 창녀도 만나셨으며
심지어 이들이 먼저 하나님 나라에 들어간다고 말씀하셨
습니다. 내 안에 주님이 계십니다. 보혜사 성령님의 인도
로 사람을 차별하여 대하지 않게 하옵소서.

야고보서 2:2
만일 너희 회당에 금 가락지를 끼고 아름다운 옷을
입은 사람이 들어오고 또 남루한 옷을 입은 가난한
사람이 들어올 때에

: 짐작컨대 나의 눈길은 분명 '동가홍상同價紅裳' – '기왕
이면 다홍치마'라며 아름다운 옷을 입은 쪽으로 갔을 것
입니다. 속물俗物이지요. 여러분은 어떻습니까?

야고보서 2:3
너희가 아름다운 옷을 입은 자를 눈여겨 보고 말하
되 여기 좋은 자리에 앉으소서 하고 또 가난한 자에
게 말하되 너는 거기 서 있든지 내 발등상 아래에

앉으라 하면

: 역지사지易地思之하여 내가 가난한 자의 처지에서 이런 모욕적인 대우를 받았다고 가정假定해 봅시다. 기분이 어떠할까요? 부와 가난을 기준으로 사람을 차별하지 않도록 나를 인도해 주십시오.

야고보서 2:4
너희끼리 서로 차별하며 악한 생각으로 판단하는 자가 되는 것이 아니냐

: 그리스 크레타에서 나고 묻힌 니코스 카잔차키스는 그의 저서 『그리스인 조르바』를 통해 '사람은 다 다르고, 각자 있는 그대로 받아들여야 해요.'라고 말합니다. 하나님 형상대로 빚어진 우리는 차별이 아니라 서로 사랑해야 합니다. 하나님은 사랑 그 자체이기 때문입니다.

야고보서 2:5
내 사랑하는 형제들아 들을지어다 하나님이 세상에서 가난한 자를 택하사 믿음에 부요하게 하시고 또 자기를 사랑하는 자들에게 약속하신 나라를 상속으로 받게 하지 아니하셨느냐

: 믿음이 충만한 사람이 되게 해 주십시오. 어려운 이웃을 사랑하는 사람이 되게 해 주십시오. 오직 감사함으로 하나님께 영광 돌리게 하십시오. 예수님 이름으로 기도합니다. 아멘

야고보서 2:6
너희는 도리어 가난한 자를 업신여겼도다 부자는 너
희를 억압하며 법정으로 끌고 가지 아니하느냐

: 빈곤은 태만의 결과일까요? 아니면 환경이 원인일까요?
가난은 그들의 탓이라고 비아냥거린 적이 있습니다. 가난
한 자를 무시한 적이 있습니다.
주님, 업신여김을 회개하니 용서해 주세요.

야고보서 2:7
그들은 너희에게 대하여 일컫는 바 그 아름다운 이
름을 비방하지 아니하느냐

: 구화지문口禍之門이라는 말이 있습니다. 입은 재앙을 불
러들이는 문이란 뜻이지요. 부자의 비유 말씀(약 2:6-7)
을 통해 나는 어떠한지 다시 돌아보게 하시는 주님, 감사
합니다.

야고보서 2:8
너희가 만일 성경에 기록된 대로 네 이웃 사랑하기
를 네 몸과 같이 하라 하신 최고의 법을 지키면 잘
하는 것이거니와

: 설교는 하나님의 말씀을 알기 쉽게 전하는 것이어야 합
니다. 우리의 기억에 남는 것은 설교자의 자기 자랑이 아
니라 하나님의 말씀이어야 합니다. '오직 성경으로(Sola
Scriptura)' - 말씀을 듣고 실천하여 세상에서 승리하게 하옵소서.

야고보서 2:9
만일 너희가 사람을 차별하여 대하면 죄를 짓는 것
이니 율법이 너희를 범법자로 정죄하리라

: 살인하고 도둑질하는 것만이 죄가 아닙니다. 사람을 차
별하여 대하는 것 - 그것이 죄라고 말씀하십니다. '죄의
삯은 사망'(롬 6:23)입니다. 그러니까 사람을 차별하고
편애하면 안되겠지요? 죄로부터 자유로워야 발을 뻗고 편
히 잡니다. 샬롬

야고보서 2:10
누구든지 온 율법을 지키다가 그 하나를 범하면 모
두 범한 자가 되나니

: '바늘 도둑이 소 도둑 된다'는 속담이 있습니다. 작은
것 하나쯤이야 하며 어기면 큰 것을 쉽게 어기게 됩니다.
이 정도는 괜찮겠지라는 생각을 버려야 합니다. 하나님의
법을 온전히 지키는 자 되게 하옵소서.(시 119:44)

야고보서 2:11
간음하지 말라 하신 이가 또한 살인하지 말라 하셨
은즉 네가 비록 간음하지 아니하여도 살인하면 율법
을 범한 자가 되느니라

: 법法은 어느 하나라도 지키라고 있는 것입니다. 사무엘
을 기다리지 못하고 망령되이 제사를 지낸 사울왕을 보십
시오. 내 멋대로 해석하여 행동하면 안 되지 않습니까?

하나님의 의로운 규례들을 지키는 것이 참 자유를 얻는
길임을 깨우쳐 주시니 감사합니다.

야고보서 2:12
너희는 자유의 율법대로 심판 받을 자처럼 말도 하
고 행하기도 하라

: 입만 열면 거짓말이요, 표리表裏가 부동不同한 행동으로
덧입혀진 범법자가 리더랍시고 득시글대는 세상입니다.
반면교사反面敎師 삼아 나는 어떤지 돌아보게 하시니 감사
합니다. 정신 똑바로 차리고 살게 하여 주십시오.

야고보서 2:13
긍휼을 행하지 아니하는 자에게는 긍휼 없는 심판이
있으리라 긍휼은 심판을 이기고 자랑하느니라

: 긍휼(矜恤, Compassion)은 '가엽게 여겨서 돕는 것'이란 뜻
입니다. 돌아온 아들의 목을 안고 입을 맞춘 아비의 마음
이지요.(눅 15:20) 맹자孟子 선생의 측은지심惻隱之心이 연
상되네요. 우리 모두 사람의 기본은 지키고 살았으면 좋
겠습니다.

야고보서 2:14
내 형제들아 만일 사람이 믿음이 있노라 하고 행함
이 없으면 무슨 유익이 있으리요 그 믿음이 능히 자
기를 구원하겠느냐

: 나의 마음속에 사랑이 있노라 하고 그 속에 자랑만 가득하면 무슨 유익이 있겠습니까? 그 자랑이 능히 나를 구원하겠습니까? 주님, 가식假飾의 늪에서 나를 건지소서.

야고보서 2:15-16
만일 형제나 자매가 헐벗고 일용할 양식이 없는데 너희 중에 누구든지 그에게 이르되 평안히 가라, 덥게 하라, 배부르게 하라 하며 그 몸에 쓸 것을 주지 아니하면 무슨 유익이 있으리요

: '학철부어涸轍鮒魚'라는 고사성어가 있습니다. '수레바퀴 자국에 괸 물에 있는 붕어'란 뜻으로 당장의 궁핍함을 표현한 말이지요. 도움은 필요한 즉시 주어야지 시간이 지나면 아무 쓸모 없습니다. 도와달라 손 내미는 곳에 바로 반응하는 양심을 주옵소서.(마 25:40, 캐럴 O Holy Night)

야고보서 2:17
이와 같이 행함이 없는 믿음은 그 자체가 죽은 것이라

: "회개하라 천국이 가까이 왔느니라" (마 4:17) 아멘

야고보서 2:18
어떤 사람은 말하기를 너는 믿음이 있고 나는 행함이 있으니 행함이 없는 네 믿음을 내게 보이라 나는

행함으로 내 믿음을 네게 보이리라 하리라

: 나는 과연 어느 쪽일까 생각합니다. 입술로만 떠드는지 아니면 가슴과 손과 발이 같이 움직이는지. 여러분은 어떻습니까? 주님, 행함으로 내 믿음이 드러나게 인도하소서.

야고보서 2:19
네가 하나님은 한 분이신 줄을 믿느냐 잘하는도다 귀신들도 믿고 떠느니라

: '사과는 왜 땅으로 떨어질까?' – 엉뚱한 질문입니다. 그러나 거기에 진리가 있습니다. 질문으로 성화聖化되게 하시고 아멘으로 하나님과 동행하며 믿음이 더욱 강화强化되는 복을 주십시오.

야고보서 2:20
아아 허탄한 사람아 행함이 없는 믿음이 헛것인 줄을 알고자 하느냐

: 믿음이면 충분하지 않습니까? 무엇이 더 필요합니까? 이런 나의 의심을 간파한 듯 친절하게 설명합니다.(약 2:21)
주님, 나에게 지혜를 주셔서 허탄한 사람이 아니라 튼실한 사람이 되게 해 주십시오.

야고보서 2:21
우리 조상 아브라함이 그 아들 이삭을 제단에 바칠 때에 행함으로 의롭다 하심을 받은 것이 아니냐

: 아브라함이 그의 아들 이삭을 제단에 바친 이야기가 당시 풍습에 따른 설화說話일까요 아니면 믿음으로 행한 실화實話일까요? 복음에 숨겨진 진리를 깨닫게 하소서.

야고보서 2:22
네가 보거니와 믿음이 그의 행함과 함께 일하고 행함으로 믿음이 온전하게 되었느니라

: 결국 믿음과 행함은 양립兩立하는 것이 아니라 서로 융합融合되어야 한다는 것입니다. 나도 믿음과 행함이 조화를 이루어 온전하게 되기를 기도합니다.

야고보서 2:23
이에 성경에 이른 바 아브라함이 하나님을 믿으니 이것을 의로 여기셨다는 말씀이 이루어졌고 그는 하나님의 벗이라 칭함을 받았나니

: '이신칭의以信稱義'는 말 그대로 '믿음을 통해 의롭다고 인정을 받는다'라는 의미입니다. 아브라함의 믿음을 통해 하나님의 전적인 은혜가 얼마나 중요한지를 배웁니다. 범사에 감사하게 하소서.

야고보서 2:24
이로 보건대 사람이 행함으로 의롭다 하심을 받고
믿음으로만은 아니니라

: 야고보 사도는 계속하여 실천을 강조하고 있습니다.
그 당시나 지금이나 언행불일치言行不一致가 참 많았나 봅
니다. 나에게 주어진 소중한 시간을 믿음으로 행하여 잘
했다 칭찬받는 성도 되게 하소서.

야고보서 2:25
또 이와 같이 기생 라합이 사자들을 접대하여 다른
길로 나가게 할 때에 행함으로 의롭다 하심을 받은
것이 아니냐

: 믿음의 여인 기생 라합의 의롭고 용기 있는 행동을 통
해 모두가 'No'할 때 'Yes'라고 말할 수 있는 결단을 다
집니다. 그 당당함이 알을 깨고 나올 수 있는 개혁의 마
인드Mind입니다. 말씀을 통해 깨닫게 하시니 감사합니다.

야고보서 2:26
영혼 없는 몸이 죽은 것 같이 행함이 없는 믿음은
죽은 것이니라

: 예배는 예배답게 하는 것이지 자기도취에 빠져 허탄한
말로 길게 하는 것이 아닙니다. 그 유명한 게티스버그 연
설을 보세요. 에버렛(Edward Everett)의 2시간짜리 연설은

잊혔지만 3분이 채 되지 않는 링컨의 연설은 불멸이 되어 지금까지도 회자되고 있지 않습니까? 하나님은 우리가 침묵할 때 말씀하십니다. 오늘은 각자가 각각 처한 곳에서 스스로 생각해 보는 시간을...
샬롬~

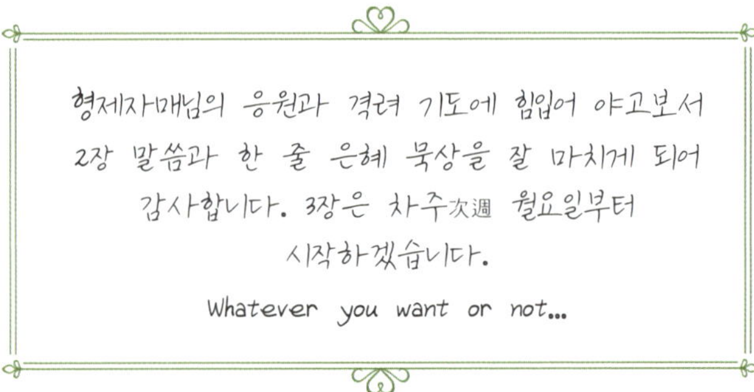

야고보서 3장

야고보서 3:1
내 형제들아 너희는 선생된 우리가 더 큰 심판을 받을 줄 알고 선생이 많이 되지 말라

: "한국 교회, 목회자 늘고 성도 줄었다. 주요 장로교단 교세 통계 다음세대 감소 비율 뚜렷"_기독신문 2020-10-13 성도가 늘어야 할 텐데 참 아이러니Irony하다는 생각은 나만의 기우杞憂일까요? 만인사제론을 주창主唱한 루터는 어떤 생각을 할까요? 기도가 답쏨입니다.

야고보서 3:2
우리가 다 실수가 많으니 만일 말에 실수가 없는 자라면 곧 온전한 사람이라 능히 온 몸도 굴레 씌우리라

: 말에 실수가 없는 사람이 어디 있겠습니까? 다만 반성하고 회개하고 온전해지도록 노력할 따름이지요. 주님, 남의 실수를 탓할 게 아니라 내 눈의 들보를 보게 하십시오.

야고보서 3:3
우리가 말들의 입에 재갈 물리는 것은 우리에게 순종하게 하려고 그 온 몸을 제어하는 것이라

: 성도 된 우리가 하나님의 법을 따르고 서로 사랑해야
하는 이유가 바로 이와 같은 것 아닐까요?
"서로 사랑하라 내가 너희를 사랑한 것 같이 너희도 서
로 사랑하라"(요 13:34)

야고보서 3:4
또 배를 보라 그렇게 크고 광풍에 밀려가는 것들을
지극히 작은 키로써 사공의 뜻대로 운행하나니

: 리더십Leadership이 얼마나 중요한지 비유의 가르침입니
다. 리더는 본本이 되어야 합니다. 본本이 되는 삶을 살아
야 합니다. 예수 그리스도를 닮은 올곧은 지도자가 교회와
나라와 세상을 지키게 하소서. Please...

야고보서 3:5
이와 같이 혀도 작은 지체로되 큰 것을 자랑하도다
보라 얼마나 작은 불이 얼마나 많은 나무를 태우는
가

: 세상을 살아가면서 경계해야 할 것이 참 많지만 화禍의
근원이 되는 세 치 혀만 하겠습니까? 나의 혀가 화의 근
원根源이 아니라 복의 원천源泉이 되게 하여 주십시오.

야고보서 3:6
혀는 곧 불이요 불의의 세계라 혀는 우리 지체 중에
서 온 몸을 더럽히고 삶의 수레바퀴를 불사르나니

그 사르는 것이 지옥 불에서 나느니라

: 성경에도 나와 있듯이 인생 여정에서 '말조심, 돈 조심, 술 조심'을 해야 합니다. 그 중에서도 특별히 말을 조심해야 합니다. 이것이 사도 야고보가 오늘 우리에게 던지는 메시지Message 아닐까요?

야고보서 3:7-8
여러 종류의 짐승과 새와 벌레와 바다의 생물은 다 사람이 길들일 수 있고 길들여 왔거니와 혀는 능히 길들일 사람이 없나니 쉬지 아니하는 악이요 죽이는 독이 가득한 것이라

: 칼에는 두 개의 날이 있지만 사람의 입에는 백 개의 날이 있다고 하잖아요? 때론 화를 참지 못하여 나의 혀로 칼춤을 추었음을 회개합니다. 주님 용서하여 주십시오. 악한 영을 물리치고 오직 사랑과 감사로 채워 주십시오. 예수님 이름으로 기도합니다. 아멘

야고보서 3:9
이것으로 우리가 주 아버지를 찬송하고 또 이것으로 하나님의 형상대로 지음을 받은 사람을 저주하나니

: 『지킬박사와 하이드』 이야기가 생각납니다. 인간의 이중성二重性인 선과 악의 내적 모순矛盾을 다룬 작품이지요. 나도 범인凡人인지라 때론 육담肉談과 기도가 한 입에서 나오니 이에 못지않음을 고백합니다. 주님, 용서해 주십시오.

야고보서 3:10
한 입에서 찬송과 저주가 나오는도다 내 형제들아
이것이 마땅하지 아니하니라

: AI(인공지능: Artificial Intelligence)시대에 ML(기계학습: Machine Learning)처럼 인간도 늘 감사와 사랑의 말만 하도록 우리의 입과 혀를 훈련시키면 어떨까요? 아니 선과 악,양면성이 있기에 인간인가요? 이 아침 생각에 젖습니다. 샬롬

야고보서 3:11
샘이 한 구멍으로 어찌 단 물과 쓴 물을 내겠느냐

: 자연은 그대로인데 인간은 왜 이다지도 다를까요? 평화로 포장된 건너편에 전쟁과 테러Terror와 기아로 죽어가는 어린이와 이웃이 있습니다. 아기 예수 탄생을 사모하며 나의 이웃인 이들에게 오늘 바로 도움을 행하게 하소서.

야고보서 3:12
내 형제들아 어찌 무화과나무가 감람 열매를, 포도나무가 무화과를 맺겠느냐 이와 같이 짠 물이 단 물을 내지 못하느니라

: 콩 심은 데 콩 나고 팥 심은 데 팥이 납니다. 못된 나무가 아름다운 열매를 맺을 수 없습니다. 그걸 알면서도 돌무화과나무에 포도가 맺기를 바랍니다. 과욕過慾입니다. 지나친 욕심을 버리게 하시고 주어진 것에 만족하는 마음을 주세요, 주님.

야고보서 3:13
너희 중에 지혜와 총명이 있는 자가 누구냐 그는 선
행으로 말미암아 지혜의 온유함으로 그 행함을 보일
지니라

: 나는 어떠한지 생각합니다. 지혜와 총명이 있는지. 선
한 행동을 하고 있는지. 참 부끄러운 새벽입니다. 말씀을
읽는 이유가 여기에 있으려니 그저 스스로 위안해 봅니
다.

야고보서 3:14
그러나 너희 마음 속에 독한 시기와 다툼이 있으면
자랑하지 말라 진리를 거슬러 거짓말하지 말라

: 미친 사람은 자기가 미친 줄을 자기만 모릅니다. 내가
지금 무슨 짓을 하고 있는지 어디로 가고 있는지 알지 못
하는 것이지요.
하나님, 어둠에서 빛으로 우리를 인도해 주십시오. 짠 맛
을 잃지 않은 소금이 되게 해 주십시오. 예수님 이름으로
기도합니다. 아멘

야고보서 3:15
이러한 지혜는 위로부터 내려온 것이 아니요 땅 위
의 것이요 정욕의 것이요 귀신의 것이니

: 지혜도 지혜 나름이라는 말씀입니다. 나로 인하여 주위
에 하나님이 전파되는지 생각합니다. 오히려 나 때문에

하나님을 떠나지는 않는지... 오직 선한 영으로 예수 그
리스도의 향기를 전하는 하루 또 하루가 되게 하소서.

야고보서 3:16
시기와 다툼이 있는 곳에는 혼란과 모든 악한 일이 있음이라

: 영어에 이런 말이 있습니다. 'Sometimes it is hard to avoid the happiness of others.'의역하면 '사촌이 땅을 사면 배가 아프다' 뭐 이런 뜻이지요. 신앙인인 우리는 시기와 다툼이 아니라 감사와 사랑으로 충만해야 합니다.
내가 기도하며 감사해야 주님께서 나를 감사의 삶으로 이끄십니다.(민 14:28)

야고보서 3:17
오직 위로부터 난 지혜는 첫째 성결하고 다음에 화평하고 관용하고 양순하며 긍휼과 선한 열매가 가득하고 편견과 거짓이 없나니

: 나의 생각을 앞세우는 순간 나도 모르게 하나님 앞에 서게 됩니다. 하나님의 의義가 아닌 나의 의義를 드러내려 합니다. 교만이지요. 나의 지식과 지혜는 과연 어디에서 온 것일까요?
"진리를 알지니 진리가 너희를 자유롭게 하리라" (요 8:32)

야고보서 3:18
화평하게 하는 자들은 화평으로 심어 의의 열매를
거두느니라

: 우리가 즐겨 쓰는 히브리어 '샬롬'이 바로 '화평'입
니다. 화목하고 평안하다는 말이지요. 어감語感도 참 부드
럽고 좋지 않나요? 우리 모두 즐겨 사용하면 좋겠습니다.
유대인의 민속노래 'Hevenu Shalom Aleichem(슥 9:9-10)'
을 다시 듣고 싶은 새벽입니다. 샬롬~

여러분의 열화와 같은 '아멘' 응답으로 야고보서
3장을 무사히 마쳤습니다. 하나님께 영광이요
은혜입니다. 감사드리고, 2024년 설 명절 건강하고
행복하게 보내세요. 차주次週 는 저의 미국
출장으로 묵상 보내 드리는 것을 한 주
건너뛰겠습니다. 샬롬

야고보서 4장

야고보서 4:1
너희 중에 싸움이 어디로부터 다툼이 어디로부터 나
느냐 너희 지체 중에서 싸우는 정욕으로부터 나는
것이 아니냐

: 정욕情欲은 탐내고 집착하는 마음입니다. 여리고성 점령
당시 아간의 행위를 보십시오. 탐심貪心이 결국 아골 골짜
기에서 사망에 이르지 않았습니까? 더 내려놓고 더 비워
가겠습니다.
"일어나 네 자리를 들고 걸어가라"(요 5:8) – 나에게
말씀하실 때까지...

야고보서 4:2
너희는 욕심을 내어도 얻지 못하여 살인하며 시기하
여도 능히 취하지 못하므로 다투고 싸우는도다 너희
가 얻지 못함은 구하지 아니하기 때문이요

: 아! 구하지 않으니 얻지 못하는구나! 문을 두드리지 않
으니 열리지 않는 것이구나! 사도 바울이 첫 번째 편지에
"쉬지 말고 기도하라"(살전 5:17)라고 기록한 것은 바
로 이런 까닭이구나! 날마다 나에게 귀한 깨달음을 주시는
하나님 감사합니다.

야고보서 4:3
구하여도 받지 못함은 정욕으로 쓰려고 잘못 구하기
때문이라

: 나봇의 포도원을 탐낸 아합왕이나 다윗을 죽이려 한 사
울왕이나 우리아의 아내를 탐한 다윗왕이나 모두 하나님
의 책망을 받은 사건입니다. 책망을 받아도 원망이 아니
라 회개하고 돌아서길 원합니다. 주님 나를 인도해 주세
요.

야고보서 4:4
간음한 여인들아 세상과 벗된 것이 하나님과 원수
됨을 알지 못하느냐 그런즉 누구든지 세상과 벗이
되고자 하는 자는 스스로 하나님과 원수 되는 것이
니라

: 여기서 '간음한 여인'은 '하나님을 떠나 세속의 즐거움
에 빠진 자'를 일컫는 말 아닐까요? 세상의 유혹이 몰려
와도 말씀으로 물리치고 승리하여 하나님의 귀한 일에 쓰
임 받게 하소서.

야고보서 4:5
너희는 하나님이 우리 속에 거하게 하신 성령이 시
기하기까지 사모한다 하신 말씀을 헛된 줄로 생각하
느냐

: 찬송가 185장 ‘이 기쁜 소식을’은 이렇게 시작합니다.
- ‘이 기쁜 소식을 온 세상 전하세 큰 환난 고통을 당하는
자에게 주 믿는 성도들 다 전할 소식은 성령이 오셨네’ -
나의 입술로 부르는 이 찬송처럼 성령이 우리와 함께 하
길 예수님 이름으로 기도합니다. 아멘

야고보서 4:6
그러나 더욱 큰 은혜를 주시나니 그러므로 일렀으되
하나님이 교만한 자를 물리치시고 겸손한 자에게 은
혜를 주신다 하였느니라

: 성도들이 입버릇처럼 ‘은혜, 은혜’ 한다고 ‘은혜 중독’
에 빠진 게 아닙니다. ‘은혜 사모’에 흠뻑 젖은 것입니
다. 교만과 겸손의 차이만큼 중독中毒과 사모思慕의 차이도
매우 큽니다. 예수의 사랑으로 내 마음을 채워 나로 겸손
한 자 되게 하소서.

야고보서 4:7
그런즉 너희는 하나님께 복종할지어다 마귀를 대적
하라 그리하면 너희를 피하리라

: 이 말씀을 읽고 듣고 느끼면서도 또 죄를 범합니다. 참
변하지 않는 게 인간의 성정性情인가 봅니다. 예배당에서
는 샤론의 향기인양 거닐다가 일상에서는 생선 썩은 내가
나서야 어찌 마귀를 대적할 수 있겠습니까? 나로 인하여
예수의 향기가 퍼지게 하소서.

야고보서 4:8
하나님을 가까이하라 그리하면 너희를 가까이하시리
라 죄인들아 손을 깨끗이 하라 두 마음을 품은 자들
아 마음을 성결하게 하라

: 선생님 자신이 말로 가르치는 것과 그 행함이 일치할
때 그 가르침의 효과는 매우 큽니다. 그만큼 남에게 가르
치는 대로 자신이 행하는 것이 어렵다는 것이지요. 나는
과연 말한 대로 행하고 있는지 깊은 생각에 잠기는 아침
입니다. 샬롬

야고보서 4:9
슬퍼하며 애통하며 울지어다 너희 웃음을 애통으로,
너희 즐거움을 근심으로 바꿀지어다

: 교회에서는 거룩한 모양을 하고 세상에 나가서는 욕망
대로 즐기고. 이것이 두 마음을 품은 것이고 마음을 정결
케 하지 않은 모습입니다. 풀은 마르고 꽃은 시드는 법.
하나님의 말씀으로 영원한 즐거움을 누리게 하소서.

야고보서 4:10
주 앞에서 낮추라 그리하면 주께서 너희를 높이시리라

: 어찌 주 앞에서 뿐이겠습니까? 일상생활에서도 마찬가
지 아닙니까? 겸양지덕謙讓之德의 아름다움이 세상에 널리
퍼졌으면 좋겠습니다. 한없이 크신 주님의 사랑이 우리들
작은 가슴에 흘러 넘쳐서 이웃으로 전해지길 소망합니다.

야고보서 4:11
형제들아 서로 비방하지 말라 형제를 비방하는 자나
형제를 판단하는 자는 곧 율법을 비방하고 율법을
판단하는 것이라 네가 만일 율법을 판단하면 율법의
준행자가 아니요 재판관이로다

: '비판批判'은 분석하여 평가함이고, '비방誹謗'은 헐뜯음
이며 공격적입니다. '비판'은 논리적이면서 옳고 그름을
가려 주지만, '비방'은 논리도 없고 옳고 그름이 없습니
다. 그럼 어찌해야 하나요? 하나님, 나로 구별할 줄 아는
성도 되게 하소서.

야고보서 4:12
입법자와 재판관은 오직 한 분이시니 능히 구원하기
도 하시며 멸하기도 하시느니라 너는 누구이기에 이
웃을 판단하느냐

: 오직 한 분이신 하나님을 찬양합니다. 오늘도 내게 산
소망의 이야기를 전하는 간증이 세워지게 하십시오. 예수
님 이름으로 기도합니다. 아멘

야고보서 4:13
들으라 너희 중에 말하기를 오늘이나 내일이나 우리
가 어떤 도시에 가서 거기서 일 년을 머물며 장사하
여 이익을 보리라 하는 자들아

: 사도 야고보 당시 교회는 다투고 싸우고 분열했습니다. 그 이유는 자기 의만 생각하는 욕심과 이기심 때문이요 자기 존재의 드러냄 즉 자기 자랑 때문입니다. 21세기 지금의 교회는 어떤가요? 주님 앞에서 더욱 나를 낮추고 허망한 자랑의 미혹迷惑에 빠지지 않기를 기도합니다.

야고보서 4:14
내일 일을 너희가 알지 못하는도다 너희 생명이 무엇이냐 너희는 잠깐 보이다가 없어지는 안개니라

: 잠깐 보이다가 없어지는 안개같은 우리를 잠잠히 사랑하시는 하나님, 그 은혜에 감사합니다.

야고보서 4:15
너희가 도리어 말하기를 주의 뜻이면 우리가 살기도 하고 이것이나 저것을 하리라 할 것이거늘

: 주의 뜻을 따라 살겠습니다. 주님이 이끄는 대로 따르겠습니다. 나의 자랑을 내세우지 않겠습니다. 말과 행동이 다르지 않기를 기도합니다.

야고보서 4:16
이제도 너희가 허탄한 자랑을 하니 그러한 자랑은 다 악한 것이라

: 평범한 일반인과는 급級이 다르다고 여기며 허영과 자기

우쭐에 취해사는 연예인병(요즈음 젊은이들은 줄여서 '연병'이
라고 하더군요)은 허망한 자랑에 빠져 허우적대는 가식과 기
만으로 포장된 병입니다. 신앙인에게는 더욱 위험하고 악
한 병이지요.
주님, 늘 부족한 나를 경계하고 또 경계하는 삶으로 이끌
어 주십시오.

야고보서 4:17
그러므로 사람이 선을 행할 줄 알고도 행하지 아니
하면 죄니라

: 선을 알고도 행하지 않으면 죄라고 말씀하십니다. 몰라
서 행하지 않았다면 그나마 나은가요? 하나님의 법과 뜻
을 알고 행하기 위해 우리는 부단히 읽고 듣고 기도하고
손과 발을 함께 움직여야 하겠습니다. 그렇지 않나요? 샬
롬

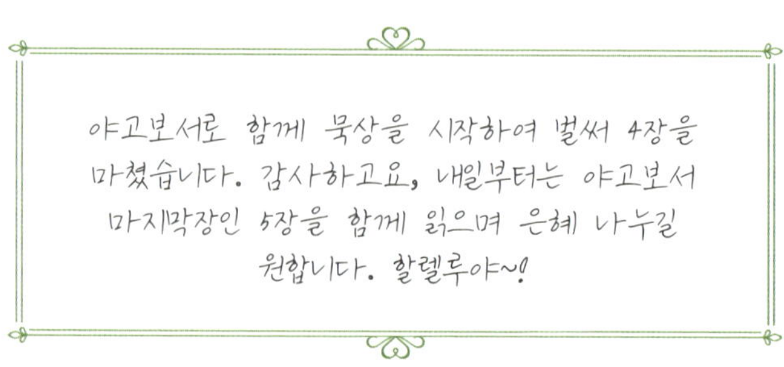

야고보서 5장

야고보서 5:1
들으라 부한 자들아 너희에게 임할 고생으로 말미암아 울고 통곡하라

: 아브라함이나 야곱이나 욥이나 큰 부자였고 심지어 요셉은 이집트의 총리까지 지낸 고관대작이었습니다. 다만 자신의 부를 하나님의 뜻에 맞게 사용했기에 구원과 천국에 이른 것이지요. 이렇게 하면 낙타도 바늘귀를 지나갈 수 있다는 소망의 말씀입니다.

야고보서 5:2
너희 재물은 썩었고 너희 옷은 좀먹었으며

: '수의에는 주머니가 없다'는 속담이 있습니다. 썩어 없어질 재물에 욕심을 내지 말라는 교훈 아닐까요? 내 것이 아니라 하나님의 것임을 인정합니다. 그러니 많든 적든 주신 재물에 감사하며 하나님의 뜻에 따라 사용해야 하지 않겠어요? 샬롬

야고보서 5:3
너희 금과 은은 녹이 슬었으니 이 녹이 너희에게 증거가 되며 불 같이 너희 살을 먹으리라 너희가 말세에 재물을 쌓았도다

: 유난히 따뜻한 2023년 겨울입니다. 빙하가 녹고 사막에 홍수까지... 미쳐 돌아가는 세상에 날씨마저 이러니 진짜 말세가 다가온 걸까요? 부자 청년의 이야기(막 10:17-23)를 곱씹어보는 하루가 되었으면 좋겠습니다.

야고보서 5:4
보라 너희 밭에서 추수한 품꾼에게 주지 아니한 삯이 소리 지르며 그 추수한 자의 우는 소리가 만군의 주의 귀에 들렸느니라

: 이런 부류의 사람을 소위 악덕업자라고 합니다. 우리는 하나님의 노여움을 두려워해야 합니다.
바빠서 잘 모르시려니 생각하면 안 됩니다. '기소불욕 물시어인己所不欲 勿施於人' - 하나님, 내가 싫어하는 일은 남에게도 행하지 않는 정한 마음을 주십시오.

야고보서 5:5
너희가 땅에서 사치하고 방종하여 살륙의 날에 너희 마음을 살찌게 하였도다

: 나의 모든 행실을 아시는 주님, 뽐내거나 자랑하거나 방종하지 않도록 언제 어디서나 나를 붙잡아 주시고 빛으로 인도 하소서.
"이는 세상에 있는 모든 것이 육신의 정욕과 안목의 정욕과 이생의 자랑이니 다 아버지께로부터 온 것이 아니요 세상으로부터 온 것이라" (요일 2:16)

야고보서 5:6
너희는 의인을 정죄하고 죽였으나 그는 너희에게 대
항하지 아니하였느니라

: 정죄가 아니라 피차 권면하길 원합니다. 정결한 마음으
로 침묵하고 기도하며 참고 기다리면 좋겠습니다. 주님,
도와주세요.
"그리스도의 말씀이 너희 속에 풍성히 거하여 모든 지혜
로 피차 가르치며 권면하고…"(골 3:16)

야고보서 5:7
그러므로 형제들아 주께서 강림하시기까지 길이 참
으라 보라 농부가 땅에서 나는 귀한 열매를 바라고
길이 참아 이른 비와 늦은 비를 기다리나니

: '기도하고 노동하고 독서하라(Ora et labora et lege)' - 몬
테카시노 수도원(Abbazia di Montecassino)을 위해 성 베네틱
트가 작성한 수도회의 생활 원칙입니다. 하나님의 축복의
비는 쉬지 않고 기도하면서 참고 기다리는 자에게 내릴
줄 믿습니디.

야고보서 5:8
너희도 길이 참고 마음을 굳건하게 하라 주의 강림
이 가까우니라

: 교회는 순결한 사람들만 모이는 공동체가 아닙니다. 알
곡과 쭉정이가 섞여 있는 타작마당이나 즙과 껍데기가 결

합된 포도알처럼 의인과 죄인이 함께 모이는 공동체입니
다.
주님 다시 오시는 날 구별이 되겠지요. 우리가 길이 참아
야 할 이유 아닐까요?

야고보서 5:9
형제들아 서로 원망하지 말라 그리하여야 심판을 면
하리라 보라 심판주가 문 밖에 서 계시니라

: 두렵지 않습니까? 심판을 망각하고 살고 있는 건 아닌
지 나를 돌아봅니다. 이웃 사랑이 아니라 나의 자랑과 나
의 욕심만을 위해 살고 있는건 아닌지.
하나님, 좁쌀 한 톨만큼의 책임이라도 느끼며 살게 해 주
십시오.

야고보서 5:10
형제들아 주의 이름으로 말한 선지자들을 고난과 오
래 참음의 본으로 삼으라

: 선지자들도 고난을 받으나 인내하는 자가 복되다고 강
조합니다. 선지자가 누구입니까? 아브라함과 모세, 사무
엘 그리고 엘리야, 엘리사 등 담대히 고난을 받으시고 인
내하신 분들입니다. 우리도 이런 삶으로 타인의 본本이 되
었으면 좋겠습니다.

야고보서 5:11
보라 인내하는 자를 우리가 복되다 하나니 너희가
욥의 인내를 들었고 주께서 주신 결말을 보았거니와
주는 가장 자비하시고 긍휼히 여기시는 이시니라

: 기독교는 고난의 종교라고 합니다. 욥의 고난을 통해
인내의 끝장을 배웁니다. 배가 부르면 쇠퇴하는 모습을
기독교 역사가 보여 줍니다. 나그네로 살아가는 벌레 같
은 나이지만 경건한 인생으로 인도하소서.

야고보서 5:12
내 형제들아 무엇보다도 맹세하지 말지니 하늘로나
땅으로나 아무 다른 것으로도 맹세하지 말고 오직
너희가 그렇다고 생각하는 것은 그렇다 하고 아니라
고 생각하는 것은 아니라 하여 정죄 받음을 면하라

: 아무것에도 함부로 맹세하지 말라는 말씀은 헛다짐을
하지 말라는 것입니다. 우리가 할 일은 그저 옳은 것은
옳다하고 그른 것은 그르다고 할 따름입니다.
"무릇 사람을 의시하는 자는 저주를 받을지어다"(렘 17:5)
– 여호와의 음성입니다.

야고보서 5:13
너희 중에 고난당하는 자가 있느냐 그는 기도할 것
이요 즐거워하는 자가 있느냐 그는 찬송할지니라

: 즐겁고 행복할 때 찬송으로 하나님께 영광을 올리게 하
시고, 일이 잘 풀리지 않고 힘들 때 시련마저 감사하며
기도로 간구하게 하소서. 악의 시험(Temptation)을 물리치고
고난의 시험(Test)을 통과해야 하나님의 선물이 있음을 믿
습니다.

야고보서 5:14
너희 중에 병든 자가 있느냐 그는 교회의 장로들을
청할 것이요 그들은 주의 이름으로 기름을 바르며
그를 위하여 기도할지니라

: 결국 기도 외엔 답이 없다는 말씀 아닐까요? 타인을 위
한 도고禱告가 얼마나 큰 힘인지 수많은 간증이 증명하고
있습니다. 기도가 필요한 이웃을 위해 지금 바로 무릎을
꿇어야겠습니다. 나 스스로를 위한 기도보다 기쁨이 배가
될 줄 믿습니다.(딤전 2:1)

야고보서 5:15
믿음의 기도는 병든 자를 구원하리니 주께서 그를
일으키시리라 혹시 죄를 범하였을지라도 사하심을
받으리라

: "믿음이 작은 자여 왜 의심하였느냐"(마 14:31) - 물
위를 걷다가 바람을 보고 두려워하여 바다에 빠져버린 베
드로의 손을 잡아주며 예수님이 하신 말씀입니다. 할 수
있을까가 아니라 믿는 자에게는 능치 못할 일이 없는 줄
믿습니다.(막 9:23)

야고보서 5:16
그러므로 너희 죄를 서로 고백하며 병이 낫기를 위
하여 서로 기도하라 의인의 간구는 역사하는 힘이
큼이니라

: 이처럼 남을 위한 기도의 힘은 위대합니다. 의인義人의
기도가 얼마나 대단한지 기억하면서 함께 중보仲保하며 기
도하길 원합니다. 내 방식이 아니라 하나님께 전권을 위
임하고 그 길을 따르게 인도하소서.

야고보서 5:17
엘리야는 우리와 성정이 같은 사람이로되 그가 비가
오지 않기를 간절히 기도한즉 삼 년 육 개월 동안
땅에 비가 오지 아니하고

: 내가 기도해도 삼 년 육 개월동안 비가 오지 않을까요?
기도해도 안 되는 건 나의 믿음이 작기 때문일까요? 간절
함이 덜해서 인가요? 아니면 나의 조급함 때문일까요? 선
지자 엘리야는 되는데 나는 왜 안 될까요? 주권은 하나님
께 있습니다.

야고보서 5:18
다시 기도하니 하늘이 비를 주고 땅이 열매를 맺었
느니라

: 얍복강에서 끝까지 포기하지 않고 날이 새도록 천사와
싸우며 매달린 야곱처럼 나도 열매를 맺을 때까지 기도하

며 기다리길 원합니다. 하늘은 반드시 비를 주실 줄 믿습
니다. 아멘

야고보서 5:19-20

내 형제들아 너희 중에 미혹되어 진리를 떠난 자를
누가 돌아서게 하면 너희가 알 것은 죄인을 미혹된
길에서 돌아서게 하는 자가 그의 영혼을 사망에서
구원할 것이며 허다한 죄를 덮을 것임이라

: 죄인을 돌아서게 하는 것은 용기가 필요한가요, 믿음이
필요한가요? 무엇이 나를 망설이게 하나요? "주의 말씀은
내 발에 등이요 내 길에 빛이니이다"(시 119:105) - 다
윗의 고백처럼 나의 삶에도 은혜의 간증이 세워지길 원합
니다. 진리를 떠난 자여, 어서 돌아오라! 할렐루야!

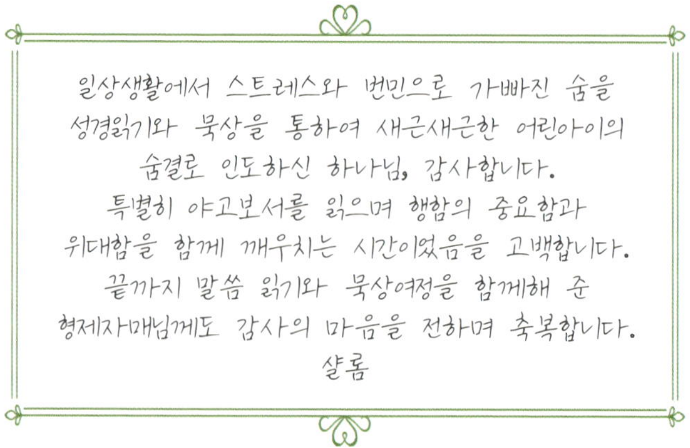

| 맺는말

작은 책일망정 두 권을 내고 나니 마음에 교만이 쌓인 걸까? 자꾸 글을 쓰고 모으고 있으니 말이다.

이 또한 욕심 아닐까? 문득문득 떠오르는 생각을 글로 옮기고 싶은 마음이 다 내려놓아야 한다는 마음을 누르나 보다.

사실 시라고 하기엔 매우 어설픈 것들이지만 그래도 쓰는 이유는 읽는 자와의 공감대가 있을 수도 있다는 생각에 행복하기 때문이다. 어? 이거 혹시 자기 합리화 아닐까?

맹자孟子에 삼년지애三年之艾라는 말이 있다. 틈틈이 적어 놓은 작은 것들을 나름 정리한 것이니 예쁘게 보아주기를 바랄 따름이다.

이 글을 읽는 모든 분들께 거듭 사랑과 감사함을 표하며, 더하여 외국 친구들을 위하여 시도해 본 영문 번역에 많은 도움을 준 ChatGPT에게 큰 신세를 졌음을 밝힌다.

2025년 12월
조 철 형
Steve Cho

다시 길 위에서
On the Road Again

초판발행 ┃ 2026년 4월 3일

지 은 이 ┃ 조철형
발행·편집 ┃ 두인
대   표 ┃ 안광학
주   소 ┃ 충북 청주시 흥덕구 풍년로111번길 11
대 표 전 화 ┃ 043)223-8747
이 메 일 ┃ mhkim10006@naver.com

출판신고 2022년10월14일 제573-2022-000050호

ISBN 979-11-9805036-6(03230)

값 15,000